D1076466

# THE CHANGING LANDSCAPE

# THE CHANGING LANDSCAPE

The History and Ecology of Man's impact on the face of East Anglia.

by

Patrick Armstrong
Ph.D

TERENCE DALTON LIMITED
LAVENHAM . SUFFOLK
1975

Published by
TERENCE DALTON LIMITED
ISBN 0 900963 53 0

Text set in 11/12pt. Compugraphic Baskerville

Printed in Great Britain at
THE LAVENHAM PRESS LIMITED
LAVENHAM                    SUFFOLK

# CONTENTS

# INDEX OF ILLUSTRATIONS

# Acknowledgements

I am most grateful to the following for permission to reproduce photographs: Abbot's Hall Museum of East Anglian Rural Life, Ipswich and East Suffolk Record Office, Cambridge University Committee for Aerial Photography, the Forestry Commission, Mr A. Millar, Mrs P. Whitehouse and the Revd. E. A. Armstrong. The remainder of the photographs are my own.

The map of the warren at Methwold is held by the Public Record Office, and the advertisement was photographed by Dr R. Colin Welch of the Nature Conservancy staff at Monks Wood Experimental Station. The geological map is based on an original in a Forestry Commission publication with permission.

I am indebted to the Geographical Association and the editor of *Geography* for permission to include the maps of heathland in East Suffolk and some text that originally appeared in that journal; also to the Council of the British Ecological Society for permission to base the map of part of Broadland on one that originally appeared in the *Journal of Ecology*. Dr Oliver Rackham of Cambridge University Botany School generously allowed a quotation to be taken from one of his publications and Dr George Peterken of the Nature Conservancy allowed use to be made of material in his superb article on Staverton Thicks. Other members of the Conservancy staff who assisted with advice and permission to reproduce material were Mrs G. Crompton and Drs Eric Duffey, John Sheail and Max Hooper—the last particularly for the maps showing the reduction in the length of hedgerows in the group of Huntingdonshire parishes. The nature of my debt to other authors will be apparent from the bibliography.

Two of my former colleagues at the Cambridgeshire College of Arts and Technology, Dr Peter Hoare and Mr Nick Goddard, read parts of the text and made many most helpful comments. Dr Ian Simmons of Durham University Department of Geography and Professor Bruce Proudfoot (formerly at Durham, now head of the Geography Department at the University of St Andrews) guided my studies while part of the material in this book was being collected for academic theses. Mrs Edith Carr drew my attention to privately held documents that were relevant to my researches; the staffs of the Ipswich and East Suffolk Record Office and other archive offices in East Anglia were most helpful.

My wife Moyra assisted in a multitude of ways during the preliminary fieldwork and with the typing.

Special mention must be made of the immense debt that I owe to my father, Edward Armstrong, who provided some of the photographs mentioned above, drew many of the thumbnail sketches and read through much of the text. More important, he it was who taught me to appreciate nature in the woods and fields and along the sea-shores of East Anglia.

P. H. Armstrong
Cottenham, Cambridgeshire
January 1975

For Moyra

# Introduction

OPINIONS differ as to which counties make up East Anglia, and at a time of Local Government reorganisation, when boundaries hallowed by centuries of acceptance are being redrawn, it is particularly difficult to be definitive. The kingdom of the East Angles in the sixth century included only Norfolk and Suffolk; the modern Economic Planning Region extends as far inland as the old county of Huntingdonshire. At certain times and for certain purposes Essex and parts of Lincolnshire have been and are included. This book is primarily about the landscape of Norfolk, Suffolk and Cambridgeshire, but from time to time the reader will be asked to look away from this "core area" towards the fringes of the region for comparative material.

Robert Reyce, writing of the landscape of the eastern counties in the seventeenth century, described it as being "void of any great hills, high mountains, or steep rocks; notwithstanding the which", he continued, "it is not always so low or flat, but . . . in every place it is severed and divided with little hills easy for ascent and pleasant rivers watering the low valleys." The effect of the Ice Age was to smear much of the surface of East Anglia with a variety of superficial deposits, and dissection by a network of rivers has broken the region into a series of low plateaus of varying sizes. Thus while there are not so very many places in eastern England that are over 300 feet (about 100m) above sea-level, the region is comprised of a mosaic of small areas differing in their soils, vegetation and landscape features, each with its own individuality.

Men at various times have used the landscape in different ways; they have parcelled it up into fields, dug into it for flints, for marl and for crag, and criss-crossed it with trackways, turnpikes, railways and modern dual carriageways. The result is a palimpsest: East Anglia is like a fragment of parchment or vellum that has been written across in many directions and by different hands.

Yet the landscape is not only a manuscript that presents a challenge to the student of local history, it is a living system. Forests have been felled, and former farmland has reverted to woodland; heath, down and dune have been grazed by sheep and by rabbits. Gravel-pits and peat-cuttings have been abandoned, become water-filled and have been colonised by communities of plants and animals. A landscape must therefore be seen in ecological terms, as an ecological system of which the human species is but one component, along with countless other organisms.

Two strands, therefore, are twined together to form the theme of the chapters that follow; a landscape's history and its ecology.

Figure 1. Coastal deposition: Orford Ness and Havergate Island at the mouth of the River Alde, Suffolk.                                                                *Cambridge University Collection*

# CHAPTER ONE

# East Anglia in the Making

"NOTHING so difficult as a beginning", the poet asserted. Indeed it is not easy to find a starting point for an account of the history of East Anglia's landscape. Boreholes have demonstrated that very ancient Palaeozoic rocks exist at a depth of several hundred feet beneath the eastern counties, but nowhere do they appear at the surface. The oldest rocks that do outcrop are the clays of west Cambridgeshire, that belong to the Jurassic system. Rivers brought fine material into the seas of 100 million years ago, and the bluish clays that provide the basis for the Peterborough brick-making industry were deposited. But these rocks are encountered in a relatively small proportion of the region and a more convenient point of which to begin a detailed consideration of the story of East Anglia's countryside might be the late Cretaceous. About 80 or 90 million years ago, much of the British Isles was covered by a sea that was warm, clear, and fairly shallow — perhaps 600 feet (about 180m) in depth. It seems possible that the nearby land masses — the Highlands of Scotland, for example, may have protruded above the waves — were waterless deserts; this would explain the almost complete absence of land-derived material in the deposits that were laid down in the Upper Cretaceous sea. In this ancient ocean lived myriads of minute organisms, many of which had shells or skeletons of limy material. When they died, hard parts remained after the soft tissues decomposed and these fragments fell to the sea-bottom contributing to a calcareous mud. These conditions persisted for millions of years and although accumulation was very gradual, many hundreds of feet of deposits were eventually laid down. They were compacted and consolidated by the weight of overlying material to form a uniform, white limestone — the Chalk that underlies most of East Anglia, attaining a maximum thickness of 1,350 feet (411m) in Norfolk. Where it crops out at the surface in south-west Cambridgeshire and near Newmarket in Suffolk it usually forms a gentle landscape of smooth, rounded slopes of light arable land or grassy sward, broken by occasional clusters or rows of beech trees.

Eventually, earth movements caused the sea to retreat and the layers of Chalk were tilted, warped and exposed to erosion for a substantial period, considerable amounts being removed.

Another submergence occurred about 60 million years ago, in the Eocene, and the eastern parts of both Norfolk and Suffolk were covered by the sea, but the sands and clays deposited by this incursion are largely hidden by later deposits. It is only around Ipswich in Suffolk and in Essex that the Eocene is found at the surface. Its presence, however, was confirmed in a boring put down in Great Yarmouth, where it was found to be resting on the Chalk at 506 feet (154m) below sea level.

For the most part however, these Eocene deposits are obscured by a layer of "crag", a type of shelly sand that underlies the light-soiled area in the eastern part of both Norfolk and Suffolk. The low sandy plateaus, separated from one another by the valleys of eastward-flowing rivers such as the Alde and the Blyth, are seldom more than 150 feet above sea level. They have acid, rather hungry soils, and traditionally supported considerable expanses of open heathland, but now that improved fertilizing techniques are available, the landscape is a mosaic of arable, with a few heath fragments, and improved grassland. The oldest of the crag deposits, found only in a small area of the Suffolk coastlands, is the Coralline Crag, which is of a light yellow colour and contains beds of almost perfectly preserved shells. The name arose on account of the abundance of "corals", and although these fossils were later identified as belonging to a quite different animal group, the Bryozoa, the name has been retained. Many of the creatures found as fossils in the Coralline Crag survive today in the Mediterranean Sea and it seems that this deposit accumulated as sandbanks in a warm, shallow sea.

Other sandy deposits, such as the Red Crag and the Norwich Crag, sometimes stained a rusty red colour, were deposited after the Coralline Crag. In 1959 a boring was drilled into these at Ludham in Norfolk, and the fossil creatures and plant remains contained in the material brought up were carefully examined. In some layers warm-water forms predominated but in others organisms now found in Arctic and sub-Arctic seas were found. It seems that temperate phases alternated with periods in which the climate was bitterly cold and although there were no ice masses in East Anglia at that time glaciers may have existed in northern England and Scotland. There were probably three such cold periods during the several hundred thousand years represented by the crags.

Of slightly later date than the crags is an interesting sequence called the Cromer Forest Bed Series; it appears intermittently in the cliffs along the Norfolk and Suffolk coasts, particularly between Sheringham and Mundesley. The exposures are interrupted for considerable stretches where they are hidden by cliff-falls, the result of the relentless attack by the waves undercutting rather friable material that forms the cliffs along much of the East Anglian coast. The succession comprises the *Lower Freshwater Bed,* which is infrequently preserved, but which consists of grey clay and peaty layers containing the seeds of fruits, the *Estuarine Bed* and an *Upper Freshwater Bed.* The Estuarine Bed contains uprooted and redeposited stumps of trees, but is best known for its mammal remains; the teeth and bones of many species of deer, as well as the remains of elephants, bears and hippos have been identified. 600,000 years ago, when this layer was deposited, the climate was evidently temperate, perhaps warmer than it is at the present time. The

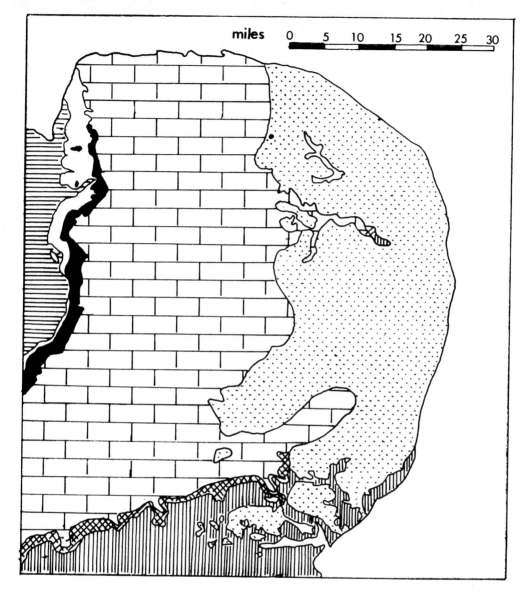

miles 0 5 10 15 20 25 30

# Geological Map : Solid Geology

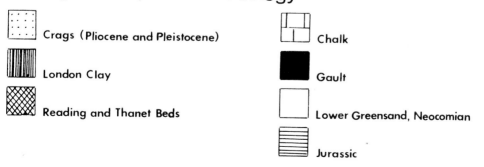

| | | | |
|---|---|---|---|
| ⠿ Crags (Pliocene and Pleistocene) | | ▥ Chalk |
| ▥ London Clay | | ■ Gault |
| ▩ Reading and Thanet Beds | | □ Lower Greensand, Neocomian |
| | | ▤ Jurassic |

Figure 2. Geological map of East Anglia, superficial deposits omitted (after Edlin)

Upper Freshwater Bed contains pollen grains from a variety of tree species; it seems that a temperate mixed oak forest with elm, oak, alder and hazel gave way to a tree community in which pine predominated, suggesting that the climate was becoming cooler. Above this is the *Arctic Freshwater Bed,* which contains the remains of plants of open tundra such as Arctic willow and birch.

As the climate grew colder, snowfields formed in the hills of northern England and Scotland; as the snow accumulated, year after year, the lowermost layers were compressed, the air expelled and glacier-ice formed. Eventually glaciers began to creep downhill along pre-existing valleys and to spread out over the lowlands. At the height of the Ice Age, ice masses covered most of Britain north of the Thames; at times the eastern fringes of the country were affected by an ice sheet from Scandinavia, for fragments of crystalline rocks — "erratics" — from the Oslo district of Norway have been found in Norfolk.

The ice advanced to cover an appreciable portion of the eastern counties on three occasions — the Anglian, Wolstonian and Devensian Glaciations. (Older books refer to the Lowestoft, Gipping and Hunstanton ice advances, named after places in East Anglia where the associated deposits are well developed.) The ice sheets plucked rocks from the surfaces over which they passed and they left behind substantial thicknesses of "glacial till", containing a variety of rock fragments in a fine-grained matrix. "Boulder clay" is the descriptive term used by earlier writers for this unconsolidated deposit. The till usually weathers to a heavy clay soil, a soil that is exceedingly tenacious when wet, and underlies the rather featureless, very gently undulating landscape of "High" Norfolk and Suffolk.

The now well-wooded ridge 300 feet or so high, stretching about 11 miles (18km) east-west from just south Cromer to Holt, was partly formed by the "rucking up" of material in the path of the Wolstonian ice sheet.

In the cliffs of the Norfolk coast, near Weybourne for example, and between West Runton and Mundesley, great contortions can be seen in the till, the result, perhaps, of one ice sheet disturbing the deposits left during an earlier glaciation. Elsewhere in the county, masses of chalk several hundred yards in length have been torn from their original positions and shifted by ice action.

Just as "warm" and "cold" layers can be identified in the crags and in deposits such as the Cromer Forest Bed Series, so it seems that "interglacials" lasting several tens of thousands of years, alternated with the full glacial stages in East Anglia. In a brickpit in the little village of Hoxne in Suffolk is a freshwater deposit of interglacial material; it occupies a hollow in till of Anglian age, and is covered by sands and gravels of Wolstonian age. The pollen found in the layers of lake deposits at Hoxne and similar sites elsewhere in East Anglia tell a story of the replacement of a scrub vegetation by birch and pine forest, followed by a period in which oak woodland predominated, and ultimately by a phase in which pine again increased as the climate deteriorated as glacial conditions approached once more.

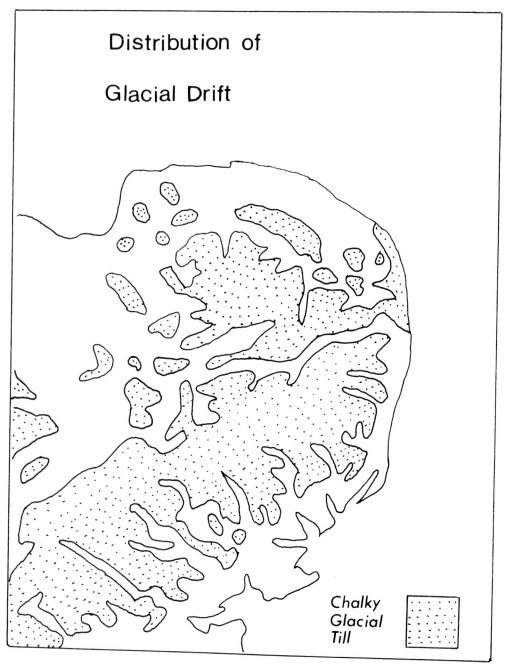

Distribution of

Glacial Drift

Chalky
Glacial
Till

Figure 3. Distribution of glacial drift in East Anglia.

Even during their retreat ice sheets had important effects on the landscape's evolution. A low ridge, referred to on some maps as Bartholomew's Hills, south of Castle Acre, Norfolk, stands out abruptly from the rather subdued terrain nearby, and may arouse the interest of the traveller making his way along the nearby A1065. Close inspection of some of the pits that have been dug into this minor eminence shows that it consists largely of sandy material, and that in places the deposits are arranged in layers; evidently it was water rather than ice that was responsible. Probably the sands are "fluvio-glacial", deposited by meltwater coming from an ice-mass immediately to the north. Furze Hill, near Hildersham in Cambridgeshire is another ridge of fluvio-glacial deposits and other features with a rather similar origin are not uncommon in East Anglia. Sometimes lumps of ice became dissociated from the main mass of a retreating glacier and were partially buried; a depression then formed when the ice melted. On occasion these hollows became water-filled and the origin of some of the mysterious meres of Breckland may perhaps be explained in this way.

During the Devensian, the most recent glacial phase, an ice-sheet only affected the coastal fringe of north Norfolk. The remainder of East Anglia, however, must have experienced an extremely severe climate; the ground was deeply and perennially frozen, except for a thin surface layer that thawed out in summer, only to refreeze in the autumn. Such an environment is described as "periglacial". Frozen ground develops vertical cracks or fissures — the process can be seen in Arctic regions today. Snow and hoar frost collect in these cracks, partially melting in the summer months. Over the years, with repeated cracking, partial melting and re-freezing, massive "ice wedges" are built up; in Alaska wedges over 16 feet (5m) across are common. When the climate improves, the ice melts and the wedges fill up with sediment. These "fossil" wedges are common in eastern England and can be seen in the sides of many sand and gravel pits and contractors' excavations; more rarely net-like patterns of fossil wedges have been preserved in such a way that they are visible at the surface or may be identified in air photographs. An elaborate pattern of irregular polygons exists in the fields of Orton Longueville parish and a few localities elsewhere in the otherwise rather featureless landscape of the Isle of Ely.

Surface patterns of rather a different type may be identified in Chalk country or on glacial deposits containing a large proportion of chalky material. In Breckland for example, patterns are frequently visible on the surface of ploughed fields as contrasting areas of chalky and sandy soil. The sandy areas are well drained and acid in reaction, while the chalky patches as well as being highly alkaline tend to be more water retentive. These differences often account for the striking contrasts in the growth of crops within a single field and variations in the character of heathland vegetation. Polygons, which are very regular in shape and frequently about 30 feet (9.1m) across, form on level ground, becoming elongated where there is the slightest slope. On slopes between ½° and about 5° the network of polygons gives way to a pattern of stripes. Many of the areas of heathland around

Thetford in Norfolk display a pattern in which the edges of polygons are picked out by heather (*Calluna vulgaris*), the chalky interiors supporting a grassy community. Save that the structures that give rise to these markings developed under severe periglacial conditions, their mode of origin is uncertain.

Figure 4. Vegetation stripes and polygons formed by periglacial disturbance of the soil at **Weeting** Heath, Breckland. Forestry Commission conifer plantations in background.

*Cambridge University Collection*

The complex sequence of alternating warm and cold periods had far-reaching consequences. Not only does the inland landscape of East Anglia bear the stamp of the Ice Age almost wherever one looks, the effects on the coast were also significant. During the glacials—there were about seven cold phases altogether, but in the first three or four, glaciers failed to reach East Anglia—an appreciable proportion of the world's waters was locked up in the ice masses. At these times the sea-level must have been lowered, rising again during the interglacials. However, the great weight of the ice sheets depressed the land somewhat, rather as though the land-masses were rafts supported by a semifluid substratum, and the removal of the burden at the end of a glacial phase allowed the land to recover. There have therefore been a complex series of oscillations in the height of sea-level over the last two million years or so, although the general trend in east and south-east England over the last few thousand years has been one of a gradual rise in the level of the sea relative to the land. The long Suffolk estuaries—those of the Deben, Orwell and Stour—with their gently sloping sides fringed with mud-flats at low tide, are submerged river valleys.

Figure 5. Coastal erosion: cliffs at Trimingham on the north Norfolk coast.

The effect of wave-attack on cliffs is evident at many points around the coasts of Norfolk and Suffolk, and the near-vertical faces cut from the Chalk at Hunstanton or the till near Cromer stand in sharp contrast to the almost imperceptible gradients of the saltings adjoining the estuaries. On the cliff-top at Dunwich a few lichen-encrusted gravestones protrude from a clutching tangle of brambles. They are all that remain of All Saints' Church, the building itself having disappeared into the sea several decades ago. Sitting at this lonely but beautiful spot, with its splendid views along the Suffolk coast, the visitor may find it hard to convince himself that the tiny hamlet behind him represents the remains of the western suburbs of a thriving mediaeval town. In the reign of King John, Dunwich was a gated town with a market and nine churches on a hill 40 feet (about 12m) above the sea. Two churches had vanished by 1300 and a spectacular advance of the sea on 14th January, 1329, choked the harbour and deflected the Dunwich River a couple of miles to the north. In 1677 the market place had disappeared; the town's western gate fell down the cliffs in 1968-9. About 1,300 feet (400m) has been removed since 1587; last century the average annual rate of loss at Dunwich was estimated at 18½ in. (47cm). But at Covehithe, about 8 miles north of Dunwich, it is recorded that wave attack removed 130 feet (40m) between August 1878 and May 1882; between 1878 and 1887 the recorded loss was 172 feet!

Probably some of the pebbles released by the erosion of the cliffs at Dunwich find their way southwards, under the influence of "beach drift", and eventually form part of Orford Ness, a blade-shaped shingle spit originally formed at the mouth of the River Alde, that extends 11 miles (18km) southwards from Aldeburgh. Waves generated by winds from the north-east are most influential in transporting beach material along the Suffolk coast, as winds from the west and south-west blow offshore and have little effect. Thus pebbles tend overall to be moved southwards as they are dragged up and down the beach by breaking waves; this continual southward march of material has been responsible for the development of Orford Ness over several centuries. The growth of this, the largest of the shingle spreads on the east coast, has been described on the basis of the evidence, some of it fragmentary, of a series of old maps, the earliest dated about 1530. The spit seems to have grown south as far as Orford by the Middle Ages, and remained approximately the same length, the Alde reaching the sea just south of the little port, for several centuries. Between 1601 and 1897 growth amounted to 2½ miles (4km), but in the latter year a great storm cut off over a mile at the southern end, throwing up large piles of pebbles at Shingle Street, on the mainland.

Blakeney Point, on the Norfolk coast, may have formed in a broadly similar way, but this structure, almost handlike in outline because of its landward-pointing lateral ridges, has grown towards the west, as beach material tends to be moved in that direction along the north coast of East Anglia. In the sheltered bays on the landward side of structures such as Blakeney Point and Orford Ness, silt has been deposited and stabilised by saltmarsh plants such as samphire (*Salicornia*) and sea

Figure 6. Orford Ness and Havergate Island, Suffolk—a landscape of shingle spit, saltmarsh and farmland.

purslane (*Halimione portulacoides*). These plants are followed by a succession of other species and a mature saltmarsh has a varied vegetation including many attractive flowering species. It is the broad expanses of purple provided by the sea lavender (*Limonium vulgare*) as well as the curves and angles of the boats on the muddy creeks between them that account for the popularity of the north Norfolk and Suffolk coasts with artists.

East Anglia has been in the making for some hundred million years. Some of the processes that have sculpted the low hills, valleys and sea-coasts can be seen at work today; others are no longer active. The physical landscape is the result of the interplay of a host of factors, some constructive, others destructive. Chalk, sands and clays are inanimate and lifeless in themselves, yet they make up the East Anglia that many men love.

Figure 7. Natural regions of East Anglia; subdivisions are as follows:

1) Fenland
2) East Norfolk sandy belt
3) Good sands
4) North Norfolk coastlands
5) Cromer ridge
6) Norfolk loams
7) Norfolk Broads
8) Breckland
9) Glacial till plateau of High Suffolk and Norfolk
10) Suffolk Sandlings
11) Chiltern Hills
12) London Basin

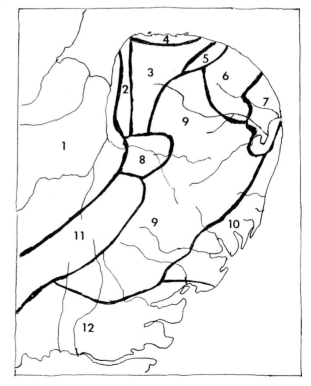

# CHAPTER TWO

# Man takes a Hand

THE HISTORY of the changing pattern of vegetation in East Anglia, as has already been hinted, has been ascertained primarily through the study of plant remains preserved in lake clays and peaty deposits. Scrutiny of the fruits, seeds and fragments of bark and wood found in successive layers can reveal the changes that have taken place in the area surrounding the site. Pollen grains, although small, vary markedly in their shape and ornamentation from one species of plant to another. They are also very resistant to decomposition and may be extracted from deposits in which other plant material is absent and identified by microscopic examination. Sometimes the pollen record can be linked with archaeological evidence — that of the distribution of finds of stone axes or the remains of former settlement sites.

Man has probably been playing at least a minor role in the evolution of East Anglia's landscape and vegetation intermittently for 400,000 years. (Even this may be an underestimate; some enigmatic flints that appear to some archaeologists to have been artificially knapped have been found in the crag deposits, but these have not universally been accepted as artefacts.) Certainly small parties of men were present in Suffolk at the time of the interglacial represented by the deposits at Hoxne. Probably groups of semi-nomadic hunters wandered through the forest in pursuit of game such as deer and the straight-tusked elephant (*Palaeoloxodon antiquus*). They settled temporarily at sites such as that by the lake-side at Hoxne, from which Old Stone Age (Lower Palaeolithic — Acheulian culture) artefacts have been recovered. Although substantial numbers of Palaeolithic implements have been found, for example in the valleys of the Great Ouse river system — the Ouse itself, the Cam, Lark, Kennet and Little Ouse — the overall density of population was probably extremely low and the total human impact on the environment small. The tools found represent a proportion of those lost or abandoned over many millennia. However, the Hoxne deposits contain a layer in which there is a reduction in the proportion of tree pollen, and an increase in that of herbaceous plants, the result maybe, of accidental burning of the forest or perhaps an attempt at deliberate clearing. Another interpretation is that the clearance was the result of a natural forest fire started by lightning.

Following this long temperate period, the climate again became colder and the Wolstonian (Gipping) ice sheet advanced across East Anglia from the north-west, and, as the late R. Rainbird Clarke put it: "The Acheulian—Clactonian hunters retreated southwards following the animals on which they preyed, leaving the tundra to the mammoth and the woolly rhinoceros."

The warm period that followed the Wolstonian ice advance has been called the Ipswichian interglacial; deposits attributable to it have been studied at Bobbitshole near Ipswich and Bruden, near Sudbury. Pollen analysis suggests that this part of Suffolk was a grassy plain with scattered patches of woodland in which hornbeam (*Carpinus betulus*) was an important component. The open areas were grazed by wild horses, while in the woods the hunters might have encountered the fearsome aurochs or wild ox (*Bos taurus primigenius*) and the giant Irish deer (*Megaceros giganteus*)—the male of the latter species had antlers 10 feet (3m) across and weighing 100 lbs (45kg). The European freshwater tortoise (*Emys orbicularis*) lived in the pools and marshes. The way of life of the hunters was not very different from that of the hunters of the earlier interglacial, but their flint-knapping techniques were quite distinctive.

Once more an ice-sheet advanced, the broad-leaved tree species giving way to pine and eventually to open tundra; once more the population, such as it was, moved away. Then about 10-12,000 years ago, the climate improved and the post-glacial (or Flandrian interglacial—there is no guarantee that the most recent glacial phase will be the last ), began. Initially the vegetation changes were similar to those of earlier interglacials. Park-tundra, made up of species such as arctic willow (*Salix herbacea*) dotted with copses of birch probably covered the eastern counties as the ice mass retreated northwards. The pollen record for sites such as that at Hockham Mere, Norfolk shows how pine succeeded birch, to be followed by warmth-demanding species such as the oak, elm and hazel about 6,000 B.C. The lime (*Tilia*), which requires even higher temperatures, became established, along with alder (*Alnus*) a little later. The more recent changes in the vegetation, however, are without parallels in the earlier interglacials.

\*     \*     \*     \*     \*     \*

About 3,000 B.C. there was a dramatic decline in the elm. Some authors have attributed this to climatic change; disease, perhaps something akin to Dutch elm disease which did so much damage to the elms of eastern and central England in the early 1970s has also been suggested. But the precise date of the "elm decline", although often sudden, varies by several centuries on either side of 3,000 B.C. in different parts of Britain and the adjacent parts of the continent of Europe. (Many samples have now been dated by the radiocarbon technique, in which the estimation of the proportion of the isotope carbon-14 in a fragment of wood or other organic material can give a good indication of the time that has elapsed since it was part of a living organism.) If either climatic change or the sudden spread of a virulent fungal infection were responsible, one might expect the dates to fall closer together. It is interesting that this decline is coincident with the start of the

Neolithic (New Stone Age) cultural phase and the beginnings of agriculture in Britain. The elm decline is generally associated with a rise in such plants as the ribwort plantain (*Plantago lanceolata*) which almost inevitably accompanies human disturbance of the soil. At Shippea Hill in the Fens the decline coincides with a Neolithic layer of bones, flints and charcoal, dated at about 3,400 B.C. It is now thought certain that the decline in the elm was due to human activity; but the question arises, why should the elm be selected for clearance in preference to other species of tree? One suggestion is that the elms had their bark removed for use as a source of fibre. Another interesting possibility is that elm leaves are particularly nutritious and that boughs were cut on a substantial scale as a source of food for stock. Archaeological evidence for a Neolithic type of animal husbandry of this sort has been found in Denmark and Switzerland.

Neolithic farmers may have used methods not dissimilar to the "swidden" or "slash and burn" cultivation still employed in remote parts of the Malaysian and South American forests—swidden is in fact an old English dialect word meaning "burnt clearing". An area of forest is felled, the boughs of the trees being burnt and crops planted in their ashes; yields fall after a few years and the cultivators move elsewhere. Traces of temporary clearings have been found in the pollen record in many parts of Europe; the sequence is as follows. There is an initial abrupt decline in oak and elm pollen, accompanied by an equally rapid rise in bracken (*Pteridium aquilinum*), plantain, dandelion, grasses and other weeds; small quantities of cereal pollen also come in. An increase in birch is also significant, as it is a "secondary" tree and it has been suggested that on fertile soils birch succeeds mixed oak forest only after burning. Later the tree-cover is restored.

There were formerly many who doubted whether substantial areas of woodland could be cleared using only the crude stone axes which were in use in the Neolithic, and so a group of Danish ecologists and archaeologists conducted an experiment. Permission was received for a hectare (about 2 acres) of Draved Forest in south Jutland to be cleared, using Neolithic methods as far as possible, in September 1953. A number of flint axe-heads were obtained from the National Museum in Copenhagen and were fitted to ashwood hafts modelled on that of the famous Sigerslev axe found in a Danish bog. Two professional lumberjacks who were recruited to assist with the felling were unable to shake off the habits of a lifetime, and used the Neolithic replicas as though they were modern steel felling-axes. They swung them "from the shoulder" and aimed powerful blows at the tree-trunks, breaking several of the ancient axe-heads. The scientists then took over the task of tree-felling themselves and found that with short, quick strokes, using elbow and wrist they were able to fell a tree with a trunk diameter of over a foot in half an hour. The area was cleared quite quickly and without difficulty, the largest trees being barked and allowed to stand. The fallen trees were permitted to remain on the ground for several months to dry out and then the tangle of fallen vegetation was burnt the following May. Primitive varieties of wheat and barley were planted in the barely cool ashes, and also in a "control" plot that was cleared but left unburnt. The cereal planted on the burned ground produced an excellent crop, later harvested with a Neolithic stone sickle. (However the following year the yield declined considerably — this would explain the temporary use of the clearings.) On the unburnt area the wheat and barley hardly grew at all. The succession of plants on the burned area — plantains, dandelions and birch seedlings — was in many ways analogous to that noted in the pollen record of the stone age clearances.

The Neolithic density of population in Breckland may well have been higher than elsewhere in East Anglia. At Grime's Graves, near the village of Weeting, Norfolk, a flint-mining industry persisted for several centuries around 2,000 B.C. Bell-shaped pits about 20-40ft (7-12m) deep were dug through the surface layers and into the chalk beneath. An elaborate network of galleries spread outwards from these shafts at the level of the layer containing the flints. Up to nine galleries have been identified as being worked (with the aid of antler axe-picks) from one pit. The total area affected by mining is about 34 acres (13.75 ha) and the infilled shafts of some 366 pits have been discerned in one area of 16 acres. Obviously flint-mining was an industry of some consequence. Although the actual number of men employed in winning the flint at any one time might have been small, they would have depended for their food and tools (antler picks for example) on a nearby population of farmers and hunters.

It is likely that flints from Grime's Graves were used to make axes employed in the clearance of the forests that formerly covered Breckland. The deep muds of the former Hockham Mere, in north-east Breckland tell a story of the vegetation changes that occurred from the late glacial until post-Tudor times. An analysis of the pollen preserved in these lake clays provides evidence of an abrupt change in the vegetation in the Neolithic. The amount of tree pollen declined, while that of ribwort plantain, ling and herbs normally thought of as being weeds of disturbed ground, such as dock (*Rumex*), increased significantly. In Breckland, it seems, a density of population rather higher than elsewhere, and the resultant heavier grazing by domestic animals, prevented the regeneration of woodland on the abandoned plots. Thus were formed the sandy heaths of south-west Norfolk and the adjoining part of Suffolk.

In other places in East Anglia the woodland persisted. From time to time evidence for the existence of these prehistoric oak forests is pulled from the dark peat of Fenland. For some years a huge trunk of "bog oak" that a farmer had found in the soil of one of his fields lay by a country road just west of Burwell in Cambridgeshire. And recent diggings at Woodwalton Fen Nature Reserve revealed many black-brown oak tree-trunks that had remained hidden in the peaty subsoil for thousands of years. Usually the bog oak wood, preserved from decomposition in the peat, decays quite quickly on exposure to the atmosphere, but sometimes it is sufficiently resilient to be used for making gate-posts or even small items of furniture. Dr. E. A.

R. Ennion, in his account of Adventurers' Fen, said that many of the ancient trees in the Fenland peat lay in the same direction, the tops of the trees towards the north-east, as if some primaeval storm had blown them all down at once!

Woodland surrounding the early clearings was affected by man's activities in a number of ways. The local removal of the forest allowed light to enter and this may account for the expansion of the ash (*Fraxinus excelsior*). This is a familiar enough tree in the hedgerows and coppices of East Anglia today, but is a species that was never really successful prior to the disturbance of the forests by Neolithic man. Lime on the other hand declined, as the inner bark or "bast" of this species was utilised as a source of fibre and probably this species was, like the elm, selectively felled.

In lonely heathland settings in the east Suffolk Sandlings the traveller may come upon a group of rounded eminences, perhaps partly covered with bracken and flanked by a small cluster of Scots pine trees. These *tumuli*, as they are called on Ordnance Survey maps, are round barrows, Bronze Age burial mounds; they have been compared to upturned pudding-basins and are typically about 12-15 feet high and 50-60 feet in diameter, although variations are considerable. As well as being common on the Sandlings heaths, they are found too in Breckland and in the Chalk country. About 250 round barrows exist or are known to have existed in the county of Norfolk and a hundred or so have been described from Suffolk — there is a group of 30 in the parishes of Foxhall, Martlesham and Brightwell in the south-east of the County. There must have been many more for frequently ploughing has flattened them and little now remains of many examples except a disc-shaped discoloration in the soil of arable farmland. The Bronze Age as a whole covers the period 1700-500 B.C., but the barrow-burial rite seems to have been important 1400-1200 B.C. Bodies were cremated and then when the funeral pyre was burnt out, the bones were collected and placed in an urn or leather bag before interment in the barrow. (It must, however, be noted that not all barrows are of Bronze Age date; a few Neolithic long barrows are to be found in East Anglia, e.g. on West Radham Common, and at Bartlow on the border between Cambridgeshire and Essex, there is a group of Roman mounds).

The distribution of these round barrows suggests that Bronze Age herdsmen grazed their stock over the lighter lands of much of Norfolk and north-west Suffolk, including the open heaths of Breckland, as well as rather similar heaths in the Sandlings of east Suffolk. There are few barrows on the clay plateau of high Suffolk, which probably remained well-wooded. As the population grew, however, an increasing proportion of the land must have been cleared. Probably the woodlands on the Chalk ridges were felled in the Bronze Age, but evidence for this is scanty, as peaty hollows or lakes in which pollen is preserved are rare on the impermeable Chalk.

Figure 8. Prehistoric burial mound or barrow; How Hill, Icklingham, Suffolk.

*Ipswich and East Suffolk Record Office*

By the Iron Age (usually defined as the period from 500 B.C. until the Roman occupation) settled agriculture was firmly established in East Anglia, although Fenland had few inhabitants. The excavation of a farmstead at West Harling in Norfolk has given much information about the day-to-day life of the farming folk of eastern England in the early Iron Age. They herded oxen and sheep and cultivated a primitive wheat—spelt. From a slightly later site at Thriplow in Cambridgeshire six-row barley was recorded. Farmland must clearly have surrounded the settlements, but seldom are field-systems of this date extant. Bones of wild boar, red deer, beaver and crane were found—hunting was obviously combined with husbandry—so expanses of forest and swamp cannot have been far away.

Figure 9. Iron age hillfort at Wandlebury, Cambridgeshire. The prehistoric encampment later became the site of a country house, now owned by the Cambridge Preservation Society. Beechwoods cover the surrounding hillsides. *Cambridge University Collection*

Other settlement sites are more impressive; in the three or four centuries before Christ there were invasions from the continent as well as considerable feuding between tribes, and some chieftains built circular hillforts. Exceptionally fine is Wandlebury Ring, set amongst beech woodland on the Gog Magog Hills above Cambridge. Part of it was excavated in 1955-56. Two circular banks, 1000 ft (about 300m) in diameter, and with a ditch between them, enclose an area of about 15 acres (6ha). The defences were probably constructed in the third century B.C., the inner bank having a timber revetting on the outside and timber supports at the back —evidence for this comes from post-holes which were found under the present, degraded bank. Perhaps in a period of freedom from inter-tribal strife, the fortifications were allowed to fall into disrepair; some of the timber facing decayed and part of the rampart collapsed into the ditch. When it was rebuilt, what remained of the old bank was scraped together and given a new timber revetting, resulting in a lower and wider bank than the original one. The ditch was recut, the earth being thrown up onto the outer bank. Later still another rampart and ditch were constructed inside the earlier one but in the eighteenth century these were deliberately destroyed to provide the mansion that had by then been built inside the Ring with more extensive grounds. At the same time a rustic walk, lined on either side with flints was constructed to run all the way round the fort in the outer ditch. This path is partly overgrown, but the ring, with its complex of banks and ditches and the Cupola Stable Block, all that remains of the country house built within it, makes an attractive venue for excursions from Cambridge. Woodland sprawls over the hillsides surrounding the Ring, partially surrounding small patches of Chalk grassland where the bright yellow flowers of the rock rose (*Helianthemum chamaecistus*) or the strange stemless thistle (*Cirsium acaulon*) with its large flower sitting in a rosette of prickly leaves may be encountered in the turf in early summer. The area is administered jointly by the Cambridge Preservation Society and the Cambridgeshire and Isle of Ely Naturalists' Trust.

Warham Camp, in north Norfolk, is in a much more open setting; the double circular rampart enclose a smaller area (3½ acres—1.4ha) than that at Wandlebury. The velvety shadows thrown in the undulating grassland in an evening light bring out the structure clearly, particularly from the air. Not far away from Warham, behind the sand dunes of Holkham Meols and less than a mile from the sea, is another Iron Age fortification—Holkham Camp—and the outworks of Thetford Castle provide yet another Norfolk example.

Up until the Iron Age the phrase "small, temporary clearings" probably accurately described most of man's efforts at agriculture. It was only when ploughs replaced digging sticks and hoes and when the importance of manuring began to be appreciated, so that land could be kept under more permanent cultivation, that the arable farmland habitat, with its bare and continuously disturbed soils became at all widespread. Plants such as the cornflower (*Centaurea cyanus*), and mugwort

(*Artemisia vulgaris*) grew in the frost-disturbed soils of the late glacial, but were almost completely suppressed by the expansion of forest, increasing once again when man began to cultivate the soil. The long association of the latter species with man is emphasised by the immense body of folklore that is attached to it; mugwort (and closely related species) has been used in witchcraft and by herbalists for many centuries in places as far apart as China, Morocco and Greece.

The change in East Anglia's life and landscape occasioned by the Roman Occupation was less than might be imagined. There was the military presence of course, and roads were constructed between the towns. But many of these urban settlements were not "anchored to the countryside" in the way that the market towns of the Middle Ages and later periods served the farmlands that surrounded them. Nevertheless, changes there were. Cultivation of parts of Fenland began soon after the conquest, wheat being extensively grown; it has been calculated that a Roman Legion would require about 500 bushels a week. Excavation of Car Dyke, in the parish of Cottenham in Cambridgeshire has shown that this canal was used for both drainage and navigation; it runs from the willow-lined River Cam at Waterbeach across a landscape of level potato and sugar-beet fields to the now embanked River Ouse. This canal, partially infilled but still used in places as a drainage ditch, was used to transport grain, via the rivers of the Fens to the military centres of Lincoln and York. Field-systems of Roman date have been identified in a number of places on the silty land of northern Fenland. At Downham West, Norfolk, where Roman pottery is frequently picked up from the fields, traces of ancient enclosures can be seen in air photographs as dark rectangles running at an angle to modern boundaries.

The Romans may also have had appreciable ecological effects. The Roman roads, with their open, sloping embankments and heavy traffic of carts laden with locally produced and imported grain for the troops, would have provided a continuous source of seeds and fruits from weeds in the process of dispersal. The scarlet pimpernel (*Anagallis arvensis*) and corncockle (*Agrostemma githago*) are but two of the many cornfield weeds that may have established themselves in the Romano-British period.

But, as was hinted above, the Roman occupation was but an interlude in the sweep of East Anglian landscape history. By A.D. 425 scrub was probably growing amidst the ruins of military towns and country houses, and a few decades later there must have been little to be seen of many former settlements but undulations in grassland. Fenland, the granary of Roman garrisons, was almost entirely abandoned on account of flooding. And in spite of the constant nibbling at the woodlands by the farmers of the later pre-historic and Romano-British periods, parts of East Anglia must still have been covered by dense oak forest when contact with Rome was lost and the legions moved away.

Amongst the earliest of English place-names, perhaps dating back to the

Anglo-Saxon invasions of the fifth century, are those that end in -ing or -ingham. The Cambridgeshire names of Dullingham, Cottenham and Willingham, mean literally the "homes of the followers of Dulla, Cotta and Wifel", and perpetuate the names of some of the leaders of the groups of invaders who moved into East Anglia southwards from the Wash, -Ing place-names are also quite common in Norfolk, particularly in some of the gravel-lined river valleys, and in east Suffolk a line of -ing settlements is arranged along the boundary between the glacial till upland and the light-soiled heathlands fringing the North Sea: Worlingham, Heveningham, Brabling, Framlingham, Bealings. They are quite absent from the heathland itself. It is as though the invaders deliberately avoided what must by then already have been open lands, preferring to make their first homes closer to where the heathland came against the closed forest, and where they would have been able to exploit both the heathland and woodland communities. From historical sources it is known that groups of Angles, by the fifth century, had made their way up-river from the Wash to establish their homes in some Midland valleys.

From the estuaries, coastlands and river valleys the descendants of these first invaders and reinforcements from across the North Sea moved onto the fertile, albeit heavy, clay soils. The plough used by the Anglo-Saxon farmers had a coulter, or mould-board, to turn the sod and was pulled by a team of eight oxen. Clearance of the forests and reclamation of the clay country proceeded apace. Confirmation comes from pollen analysis: at Old Buckenham Mere, Norfolk, Professor Godwin was able to demonstrate a substantial expansion of arable farming in Anglo-Saxon times.

Perhaps the most impressive, yet at the same time enigmatic features of the Cambridgeshire countryside is Devil's Ditch. This formidable earthwork, some 60 feet from the bottom of the ditch to the crest of the bank in its best preserved portion, runs with barely a kink in its course a full for 7½ miles (12km) from the Fenland-edge village of Reach south-eastwards into formerly well-wooded country between Stechworth and Woodditton. The number of man-days of toil required for its construction can only be guessed. It must have imposed a considerable obstacle to those seeking to move north-eastwards along the chalkland routeway. Fleam Dyke runs parallel, but is 6¼ miles (10km) to the south-west; it is only slightly less impressive. The Cambridgeshire dykes are partly overgrown by a tangled scrub of hawthorn and elder, but along considerable stretches a characteristic Chalk grassland community remains. Save for the sacred turves of the July and Beacon courses near racing Newmarket, the even-contoured land near these linear earthworks has been ploughed for barley, yet the steep slopes of the dykes have remained largely undisturbed. Here and there along these sword-straight grassy ridges rare plants grow, such as the pyramidal orchid (*Anacamptis pyramidalis*) flower, and they also provide something of an oasis for wildlife in an otherwise rather sterile landscape. In spring a walker may come upon a bullfinch or two in the hawthorn scrub, while in summer one may catch sight of the flash of the brilliant silver-blue wings of the chalkhill blue butterfly (*Lysandra coridon*). Once the writer heard the plangent"wet-me-lips" of a quail (*Coturnix coturnix*) while strolling along the crest of Fleam Dyke. This tiny migratory game-bird once bred in substantial numbers in East Anglia. Two guns took 14 quail in half a day's shooting on common land near Newmarket in 1860 and in 1870-72 were shot at Feltwell, Norfolk, but now it is extremely scarce. The whitethroat (*Sylvia communis*) a warbler with a brief staccato song, continues to build its seemingly fragile nests of a few grass stems in the low bushes that dot the steeply sloping turf of both Fleam Dyke and Devil's Ditch.

Brent Ditch, now wooded, and Heydon Ditch are similar if less monumental earthworks in the south of the county. They are parallel to the northern dykes and barred the Icknield Way. In Norfolk Bicham Ditch and the Launditch blocked movement along the east-west Roman Road and another Devil's Ditch crosses Garboldisham Heath. The Fossditch, now running through forested country in the west of the county controlled an ancient drove road. Suffolk has but few examples. In spite of many excavations, particularly of the Cambridgeshire examples, accurate dating is still impossible, and it may be that these linear earthworks, as a group, span several centuries. The Fossditch was certainly built after about A.D. 390, and none is likely to have been thrown up later than the seventh century. Nor has anyone been able to explain their purpose entirely satisfactorily. It has been suggested that they might be attributed to the period of warfare around A.D. 655, when Penga of Mercia overthrew the rulers of East Anglia, but some of the defences seem of slightly earlier date than this. Another suggestion is that they were built as barriers to cattle rustling!

\* \* \* \* \* \*

By the end of the Dark Age period man's imprint was already heavy on the land. His husbandry and mineral workings, his burial rituals and military extravagances had already left their marks. Many species of plants had probably been unwittingly introduced and certainly some animals, such as the brown bear (*Ursus arctos*), had already been eliminated (although bears survived in Scotland until the tenth century). But most important of all, man had cleared much of the woodland: before the Neolithic East Anglia could have been described as "woodland, with holes". On the eve of the Norman Conquest, although forests such as Bruneswald, between the Ouse and the Nene, remained to provide shelter for Hereward the Wake, the holes had become so enlarged that, like a woollen garment that has suffered from the voracious appetites of clothes-moth larvae, the mantle of woodland had been reduced to a scattering of separated fragments.

# CHAPTER THREE

# Woods as Historical Monuments

". . . the green woods laugh with the voice of joy"
William Blake.

THE MAGNIFICENCE of a spread of a million pale-yellow oxlip blooms on the floor of an oakwood, the brilliant blue of a drift of bluebells in diffuse sunlight, the industrious hammering of a woodpecker as it carves out its nesting hole from the fungus-impregnated wood of a dead tree-trunk — there is a particular quality about the combination of sights, sounds and scents typical of an English woodland in spring.

To someone interested in natural history it is the ecological complexity as well as the aesthetic attractiveness of a woodland that is appealing. A wood, according to the Oxford Dictionary, consists of "growing trees occupying a considerable tract of ground." But a wood may contain a dozen species of tree, and it is a complex of relationships between hundreds of species of plants and animals, an ecosystem in which each type of organism has its niche in the total scheme of things. An ecologist might divide a forest community into a series of zones — the subsoil and topsoil, the ground zone of grasses and mosses a few inches from the soil surface, the field layer (the tangle of shrubs and in some woodlands, bracken, that occupies the next six feet) and the canopy of overhanging branches and leaves. Conditions differ between these zones — the daily range in temperature, the humidity of the air, amount of light and so on — and each layer has its own complement of plants and animals. The soil will probably contain one or two species of earthworm in addition to the countless microscopic forms of life, the bacteria and fungi, on which the worms depend. The layer of organic matter on the woodland floor will contain woodlice, springtails, millepedes and other invertebrates that feed in and on the decaying leaves. In the higher strata of the forest community there are important differences in the heights at which different species of bird build their nests. A hen pheasant usually hides her dozen pale khaki eggs in a hollow amongst the fallen leaves; warblers often nest just a little above the soil in brambles thickets; a pair of mistle thrushes might set up house in a fork between branches some 15 feet from the ground, and each spring from late February onward the highest elms will have been clamorous as the neighbourhood's rookery prepared for the breeding season.

There are many links between the different layers. Tawny owls nesting in a hole in a tree 30-40 feet from the ground seek their food of mice and voles on the

Figure 10. Ecological relationship in woodland: the hole of a green woodpecker (*Picus viridis*) in a birch tree (*Betula pendula*), beneath the fruiting body of a fungus (*Polyporus betulinus*). *Forestry Commission*

woodland floor. Winter moth (*Opherophtera brumata*) caterpillars feed in vast numbers on the leaves of the trees for several months of the year but they climb down the trunk and burrow into the soil before turning into chrysalids. In the summer scorpion flies move in and out of the shrubs, occasionally dropping to the ground in search of food. The different sub-communities within the woodland ecosystem are linked to one another in a fascinating network of relationships.

Something of the ecological complexity that can exist within a quite small wood can be gathered from a consideration of the variety of organisms to be found associated with a single species of tree. There are some 227 species of invertebrate — caterpillars, mites, aphids and beetles — associated with the oak. About 50 species are associated with galls! These oak-galls (oak-apples) are the marble-like swellings half an inch or so in diameter on the twigs and leaves of the oak, made by the grub of a wasp. Oak-apples (and acorns, there is a simple elegance in an acorn resting neatly in its cup) have appealed to generations of children; Beatrix Potter's character Squirrel Nutkin played marbles with oak apples outside Old Brown's door. But they are, although so small, quite complex ecological communities in themselves. In oak-apples, the wasp responsible, *Biorhiza pallida,* may in its turn be parasitised by small creatures called chalcids, and there are likely to be other species present living on the tissues of the gall without harming the gall-former. When one adds the dozen or so species that live in acorns, the birds that nest in the branches of the oak and the squirrels and mice that depend on this tree for their autumn and winter food it is little wonder that E. T. Connold, in his monograph on British oak-galls should have observed that "the British oak is the abode of a vast concourse of dependants."

The history of the early clearance of woodland in East Anglia has already been briefly described (Chapter Two). As the result of centuries of intermittent attack, much of East Anglia's forest cover had been removed by the time of the Norman Conquest.

The Anglo-Saxon Chronicle records that following the Gloucester Gemot King William:

"... sent his men all over England, into each shire, and caused them to find how many hides were within that shire, and what the King had himself in the way of land and cattle, and ... he caused them to write down how much land belonged to his arch-bishops, his bishops, his abbots and his earls."

(A hide was a measure of land.)

The result of these enquiries was a unique inventory of the land holdings of Norman England — the Domesday Book. The book seems primarily to have been compiled for fiscal and legal purposes, although there is some dispute about this; nevertheless many of the observations recorded provide a basis for deductions concerning the pattern of land use and vegetation. Unfortunately for the modern enquirer, however, there was little standardisation in the manner in which the particulars were recorded or in the level of detail. Students of the landscape of Cambridgeshire, Huntingdonshire, Lincolnshire, Norfolk, Suffolk and Essex are fortunate in that these counties of eastern England were covered in the Little Domesday Book in much greater detail than the rest of the country, but there are tantalising omissions and countless anomalies.

The way in which woodland was recorded by King William's Commissioners vividly illustrates the problems with which we are confronted. In Norfolk and Suffolk the size of a holding of woodland was normally recorded in terms of the number of swine for which it provided pannage. Thus at Leiston in Suffolk it is noted that there was food for 200, although there were only 72 swine "and one pig" to make use of it! In Huntingdonshire the size of an area of woodland is given in linear measurements. At Woodwalton the Commissioners noted, with an accuracy typical of Huntingdonshire woodland entries, a wood 16 furlongs in length and 6 furlongs and 2 roods in breadth. Whether they were referring to the broadest dimensions or giving an average figure is uncertain. Elsewhere in the county the presence of "underwood" is noted and in parts of Cambridgeshire references to "wood for the repair of fences and houses" are included, In a few localities in Huntingdonshire the procedure adopted in much of Lincolnshire is followed and the area under woodland is stated in acres, but the relationship between a Domesday acre and its modern equivalent is difficult to quantify. In any case it seems possible that it varied from one locality to another. Sometimes two methods of recording were combined; East Dereham in Norfolk had three acres of woodland as well as woodland for several hundred swine!

Nevertheless an overall pattern can be discerned. The inland plateau of Norfolk and Suffolk, the region sometimes locally known as "The Woodland" until last century, was well timbered; there were several manors in these two counties with wood sufficient to provide pannage for over 800 swine, and at Thorpe, near Norwich there was wood enough for 1,200. (Essex was even more heavily forested; Walton is mentioned as being able to support nearly 2,400 swine.) The light sandy soils of Breckland, and, with the single exception of the substantial holding at Leiston, of east Cambridgeshire seems to have supported a considerable expanse of woodland, but in spite of occasional entries noting wood for 60 swine at Gransden and 20 at Eltisley cover seems to have been lighter west of Cambridge. There are few Domesday records of woodland in the Fens.

There is evidence that the woodlands of eastern England wasted rapidly after the Conquest. There was woodland for 500 swine at Leiston in 1066, but by the time of the survey in 1086 there was only pannage for 200. Yet the number of plough-teams seems to have fallen rather than risen during the 20 years; the record for Leiston continues: "Then on the demesne 11 ploughs, and now 7". At Burton in Norfolk the decline was from an area of woodland capable of supporting 1,000 swine to one able to accommodate only 200; the reduction was accompanied by no spectacular increase in ploughland. The picture seems to be one of "waste" rather than the deliberate clearance of woodland for cultivation. R. Lennard describes the situation well:

> "Here and there the plough may have penetrated the bounds of former wood-land. But in general the Domesday record points unmistakably, not to 'assarting' but to 'waste'. The tall trees had gone and with them the acorns and beech mast on which the pigs of the peasantry had fed. But the tree stumps, one suspects, remained and they must have been a serious obstacle to cultivation, while thickets of scrub must have taken the place of the standing timber."

(Assarting = the removal of trees and the use of former woodland for cultivation.)

The long-continued use of the woodland for the pannage of swine had probably left its mark, for this practice was detrimental to regeneration. Few acorns or beech nuts would survive to grow into saplings, and any young trees that did develop would have been at serious risk from trampling or being eaten back. Deer, too, when present, are detrimental to the regeneration of woodland; there is also evidence that cattle and even sheep were from time to time pastured in the woods of mediaeval East Anglia. But there seems no satisfactory explanation of the abrupt and spectacular reduction in the wooded area between 1066 and 1086. It has been argued that the decline in the area under the plough, mentioned above, was a form of passive resistance to the Normans, or an attempt at the evasion of their taxes. Conceivably the destruction of woodland was a similar gesture of defiance by the population against an alien occupation.

Clearly, although on the heavier, damper soils, substantial woodlands still existed, by the time of the survey much of East Anglia had been deforested. Some authors have even suggested that in certain parts of the region the proportion of land under woodland was smaller then than it is today. Dr Oliver Rackham estimates that about 2% of south-west Cambridgeshire supported woodland in Norman times.

It would be pleasing if we were able to locate precisely some of the Domesday woodlands of the eastern counties, and to trace their history down to the present. Unfortunately it is seldom possible to be certain that woodland described in more recent documents is on the same site. However, it seems possible that Hayley Wood in Cambridgeshire is the same as that mentioned by King William's Commissioners and the Nottinghamshire Trust for Nature Conservation, announced that they had acquired a fragment of "Domesday woodland" when they purchased Treswell Wood, near Retford, an area of 118 acres (48 hectares) of oak, hazel and ash. This wood, a little outside East Anglia, is unusually rich in shrub species—this is indicative of an ancient origin—besides providing a habitat for a number of rare insects, including the speckled bush cricket (*Leptophyes punctatissma*).

A range of documentary sources is available to the enquirer interested in the history of East Anglia's woodlands, subsequent to the Domesday survey.

In 1279 Edward I ordered a second national survey of land tenancy; the voluminous statistics collected were recorded as the "Hundred Rolls". Unfortunately many of the documents were eaten by rats, but students of the landscape of the eastern counties are in a privileged position, for part of the area is covered by fragments published in 1812 and 1818 by H.M. Historical Manuscripts Commission. Substantial areas of East Anglia were held by ecclesiastical foundations; by 1200 there were over 80 monasteries in Norfolk and Suffolk alone. Sometimes monastic cartularies mention management of a religious house's woodland or even give some description of an identifiable wood. Real difficulties frequently exist in the interpretation of this early mediaeval material. In a study of the areal extent of the mediaeval woodlands in Cambridgeshire, the areas given in the Hundred Rolls, and another thirteenth century source, the Ely Coucher Book, were compared with those of the present-day woods. There was a strong correlation, but in practically every case the thirteenth century area was the smaller. In most cases the difference between the two figures was 45%. Since it is very unlikely that all the woods would have increased by the same proportion, particularly as known changes had been allowed for, it seems as though the discrepancy was due to a consistent error in surveying. Dr Rackham comments:

"Considering the baffling difficulty of surveying an irregularly-shaped wood without trigonometry or the other aids of the modern map-maker, the consistency of the medieval areas is surprisingly good. Most of them agree among themselves to within 10%, which is about the accuracy to which they are quoted. Even with modern methods, it is difficult to measure an irregular area to better than ½%."

Farm accounts, leases and estate plans may still be held locally in an estate office, or may have been passed to a Local Authority Archivist for safe keeping; the East Suffolk Record Office in Ipswich and the Cambridgeshire County Archives Office at Shire Hall, Cambridge have substantial holdings of sources, which are of value in a study of woodland management in the post-mediaeval period.

Old maps are often useful, as they may allow the contraction or expansion of an area of woodland to be traced through the years. Sometimes they provide clear evidence for the continuity of woodland cover on a site for several centuries. One of the earliest maps that give a good indication of the distribution of woodland in Suffolk is that of W. Faden, dated 1783. The Ordnance Survey had its official beginnings in 1791; although inaccuracies in the First Edition exist, the neat lettering, fine hachuring and carefully picked out woods and coppices of the *Old Series,* all originally engraved on heavy copper plates, represented a substantial improvement on anything of earlier date. Much of East Anglia is covered on sheets published in 1823 and 1824. From this point onwards the history of a woodland area can often be traced in considerable detail; six-inch coverage followed about half a century later and other editions succeeded one another at fairly regular intervals. From the 1930s onwards oblique and vertical air photographs are often available.

But a study of maps and old documents, however scholarly, can reveal only an incomplete picture. The woodland historian must move from the muniment room to the countryside and seek confirmation of his theories on the ground. He must note the size, shape and spacing of old oak trees and consider the thickness and biological diversity of the shrubby undergrowth beneath them. He must look for the barely perceptible rise and fall of the ground beneath the stands of elm and ash and examine bark for the grey-green encrustations of lichens.

"Virgin" woodland that has never been cleared, is a highly complex ecosystem, a community containing countless species of mosses, lichens and fungi, insects and spiders in a delicate state of equilibrium with one another. Human interference, of whatever character — selective felling, grazing or even the long-continued collection of dead timber for firewood — results in the alteration of this balance. On the other hand if an area of farmland or pasture is abandoned, within a year or two the overgrown mixture of grasses and annual weeds will be invaded by shrub species like hawthorn (*Crataegus monogyna*). After a further decade or so the shade and shelter provided by these pioneer colonisers will allow other woodland species to follow as birds and the wind bring in seeds, fruits and berries. A cinder tennis-court was constructed between the wars on Paradise Land, an area of damp pasture near the River Cam, just south of Cambridge. It fell into disuse at the start of the Second

World War and by the late 1940s a few saplings were growing up through the hard core. Twenty five years later it had a good growth of ash and willow, some of the trees 35 feet (12m) high, with song thrushes and hedge sparrows nesting in the confusion of bramble beneath them. But many other species of plant and animal, having to colonise across miles of open country from woodland elsewhere would require much longer to return. Many would never find their way back. It is because the woods and spinneys of East Anglia are the outcome of management and felling, abandonment, ecological succession and natural regeneration that the techniques of the field naturalist must be called upon to supplement documented history.

Within certain limits lichens are good indicators of a woodland's antiquity and relative freedom from disturbance. A species called *Haematomma elatinum* was until recently thought to be confined to south-west Ireland, Wales and the Highlands of Scotland. But it was found in 1968 to be quite abundant in woodland at Staverton Park and Staverton Thicks in east Suffolk, areas that have certainly been forested since the thirteenth century, and probably for a great deal longer. It has also been discovered in a number of woodland areas which have every appearance of being stands of considerable antiquity in south-east England and the New Forest. *Thelotrema lepadinum* and *Stenocybe septata* are other rare species normally associated with old woodlands which have been found at Staverton. The area has a flora of over 60 lichens, 40 mosses and eight liverworts — highly unusual for a dry woodland site in eastern England. One note of caution must be added: lichens are extremely susceptible to air pollution, particularly sulphur-dioxide, and although in Norfolk and Suffolk the level of contamination is much lower, for example, than in South Wales, where lichen growth is seriously inhibited, it is possible that the lichen flora may be somewhat impoverished in parts of the region affected by air-borne pollution from London and the Midlands.

ure 11. Oxlip (*Primula elatior*) at Hayley Wood, mbridgeshire.                    *P. H. Armstrong*

Flowering plants typical of old-established woods include dog's mercury (*Mercurialis perennis*), oxlip (*Primula elatior*) and the Midland hawthorn (*crataegus oxyacanthoides*). Less ancient woods may contain the sycamore (*Acer pseudoplatanus*), Queen Anne's lace (*Anthriscus sylvestris*), the spurge laurel (*Daphne laureola*) and primrose (*Primula vulgaris*). In such woods ivy (*Hedera helix*) often carpets the ground and may climb aloft, sometimes even overwhelming small trees. While the ancient woods of East Anglia typically have a canopy of oak and ash, elm often predominates in areas of more recent reversion.

Local field-names may give clues to the former extent of a wood. Adjacent to Knapwell Wood in Cambridgeshire is a group of small enclosures known as Wood Close — "wood closes" cut out of woodland are not unusual in the district. Beyond this Wood Close is a larger field known as Stocking Furlong. "Stocking" means "a place of tree-stumps" or "stocks", and is another name not unusual in the area for a field near a wood. It is interesting that in the hedgerow boundaries of some of these fields occur one or two plant species normally associated with well-established woods such as dog's mercury, and the narrow-leaved everlasting pea (*Lathyrus sylvestris*)) and crested cow-wheat (*Melampyrum cristatum*).

Woods that have experienced relatively little interference, as well as containing a wide range of species of tree and shrub, have an uneven age-structure. In such a stand there will probably be a few giant oaks, several yards in girth, perhaps with rotten or partly hollow trunks, many mature trees and a gradation in age downwards to tiny saplings. Usually an appreciable proportion of the trunks will be those of dead trees. Plantations, of course, are of even age, but an intensively managed wood will probably show a distorted structure. Some age-groups will be abundantly represented, others absent. Gaps in the age-structure may mark periods of grazing or pannage in the wood or phases of partial clearance.

The age of a tree may be determined by felling it and counting the growth rings. Sometimes distinct phases can be identified in the life of a tree; there may be groups of rings packed closely together indicating a period of very slow growth, perhaps when the sapling was shaded and constricted by nearby trees, or following damage by deer, stock or at the hand of man. When growth is uninterrupted the rings are usually further apart. Climatic vagaries or insect-plagues may be responsible for irregularities in a sequence of otherwise evenly-spaced rings. Sometimes when the inner part of the tree has decomposed an average figure for the number of rings per inch for the remaining part of the tree will allow interpolation and the estimation of the approximate total age of the tree. The comparison of a characteristic pattern of broad and narrow rings in the interior of a recently felled tree (the date of the outermost ring will naturally be the year of felling), with similar patterns in, perhaps, a nearby dead trunk or long-felled stump, may enable the record to be stretched further into the past and a date for the death or felling of the enigmatic tree-stump to be deduced.

Figure 12. The results of former coppicing at Monks Wood, Huntingdonshire. This old ash (*Fraxinus excelsior*) stool is about six feet in diameter at its base. After the last cutting, seven shoots were allowed to grow uncut and now form large trunks.                    *A. Millar*

Felling a large number of trees to ascertain their ages is unnecessarily destructive. In the U.S.A. ages of trees are often determined using an instrument known as an increment borer, which removes a core of wood from the trunk, in which the rings can be counted. Tree-ring study is an important technique in archaeology in the south-western states, as prehistory includes the whole of the period prior to the arrival of the Spaniards in 1540, and Indian sites may be dated by comparing the growth rings in the timbers of their ancient dwellings with those in adjacent recently felled trees. High in the White Mountains along the state-line between California and Nevada are stands of bristlecone pine trees (*Pinus longaeva*), with their gnarled, russet-coloured trunks and battered crowns, not tall in stature, but of truly venerable age. Some are over 4,000 years old; one bristlecone felled at Wheeler Peak, Nevada was found to have 4,900 growth rings. By comparing bands in living trees with dead trees nearby — they remain in the position of growth for many centuries after death — it has been possible to carry the record back 8,000 years. It is little wonder that "dendrochronology" is regarded as important by American archaeologists.

Although very great tree-ring ages are unusual in Britain — in our damp climate wood decomposes much more rapidly than on the arid mesas of Arizona, New Mexico and Nevada — the technique is nevertheless useful. Dr G. F. Peterken counted 285 rings in the trunk of an old oak at Staverton Thicks that had died 5-15 years before his 1967 study. Both the outer sapwood and the heartwood had partly rotted, but growth in the remaining part of the trunk appeared remarkably even, and, making an estimate for the lost portion, he arrived at a figure of 420 years.

A "minimum age" for a tree may be obtained by taking a section through a branch rather than the main trunk, although allowance has to be made for the period of growth represented by the distance from the crotch to the cut. Cuts of this type might provide an indication of when a tree had last been "pollarded".

The measurement of the girth of a number of trees belonging to the same (or very closely related) species, may, if plotted on a graph or "histogram" such as those in figures 13 and 14 provide sufficient evidence for different "generations" or "regeneration phases" to be separated. It is important that a representative sample of trees be taken. One method is to extend a tape in a straight line, say, through 50 yards of the wood, and measure every tree within 12 ft of it. This is repeated for different plots until a sample of 50, 100 or preferably 250 trees has been examined. Ring-counts from a limited number of stumps may enable the very approximate dating of the generations.

Over the broad sweep of the centuries, the tendency has been for timbered land to be cleared. Robert Reyce, in his *Breviary of Suffolk,* in 1618 lamented that woodland was ". . . now nothing so plentifull as of late days" as the result of the requirements of shipping, building and wars and that "the continuall desire of Merchants in traversing all the countries and kingdoms of this inferior world for

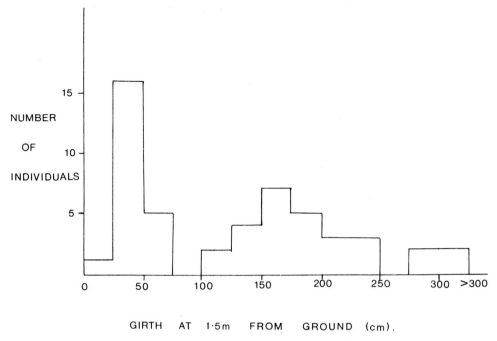

Figure 13. Histogram showing the trunk-circumference of a sample of 50 pine trees near Langmere, Norfolk. Two distinct groups can be identified: those that date from the establishment of the plantation in the late eighteenth century and those that have regenerated as the result of the reduction in rabbit pressure since 1954.

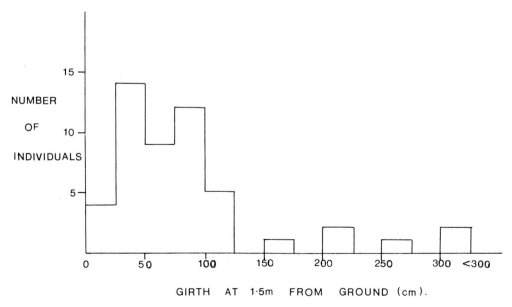

Figure 14. Histogram showing the trunk-circumference of elms in a Cambridgeshire woodland. At least three groups can be identified: a small number of trees ("standards") a couple of centuries old, well-established trees several decades old, younger saplings.

gain hath utterly consumed our timber." Arthur Young, the perceptive eighteenth century traveller, was able to record: "The woods of Suffolk hardly deserve mentioning, except for the fact that they pay in general but indifferently . . . Underwoods are not generally productive." Nevertheless, as has already been hinted, local abandonment has from time to time resulted in the reversion of former cultivated ground to woodland, sometimes adjacent to an existing wood, occasionally elsewhere.

Many mediaeval woods were surrounded by banks ; at Knapwell the wood has overgrown its original bounds slightly and has thus preserved the ancient enclosing bank and ditch. Madingley Wood in Cambridgeshire, not far distant from Knapwell, has similarly expanded beyond the ditch that surrounds its mediaeval core. Fieldwork and the study of documents have revealed a series of stages of accretion, particularly in the eighteenth and nineteenth centuries. Nearly half of the present wood shows signs of "ridge and furrow" markings in the ground, evidence of former arable cultivation (see Chapter Four).

Overhall Grove, another Cambridgeshire woodland, famous for its oxlips and bluebells, is appropriately named, for it occupies the site of a manor and in the northern part of the grove an elaborate complex of earthworks reveals the position of a former settlement, now inhabited only by a family of badgers. Close by, another area of ancient ridge and furrow is now shaded by mature oaks and elms. Although the woodland is not mentioned in the most ancient documents relating to the area, reversion seems to have taken place in mediaeval times for a map of the Boxworth manors now in the Huntingdon Record Office shows that by 1650 much of the present area of Overhall Grove was wooded. The oldest oaks in the woodland date from about 1700.

The use of woodlands as pannage for swine in mediaeval times must have had significant ecological consequences, but probably even greater in its effect was coppicing, the regular clear-felling, or much more usually, partial felling of trees as a source of timber. Typically a coppiced woodland has a three-storeyed structure; "standards", tall well-formed trees, usually oaks but sometimes ashes, maples or elms, form the uppermost layer of the canopy. There are generally about 20 to the acre; they acted as a source of acorns (or ash keys) and so assisted regeneration, and they may have protected the soil to some extent. Standards were occasionally "pollarded — the branches were lopped off leaving the main trunk untouched. Below the standards a "large coppice" layer of ash and maple can still be made out in many woods; traditionally this was regularly cut about a yard from the ground — there was some variation from wood to wood. After each cutting the "stools" threw out a number of shoots which were allowed to grow for some years before use as poles or fencing material. The layer of the canopy closest to the ground, is, in eastern England "small coppice" of hazel and hawthorn.

Coppicing was the normal method of woodland management throughout mediaeval times; there are references to *silua minuta,* thought to refer to coppice without standards, in the Domesday record for Huntingdonshire. Locally coppicing continued into the present century. It is known to have been practised in woods in lowland Britain as far apart as Huntingdonshire and Sussex, Somerset and Suffolk. Similar techniques are used in some countries on the continent.

Figure 15. Coppicing at Thorington Hall wood, Suffolk, 1922. Underwood ready for sale. In the foreground are Spanish chestnut poles; bundles of "thatching stuff" (hazel) standing against tree; in background, "faggots" or "bovins" piled in lots of 25.    *Ipswich and East Suffolk Record Office*

About 6 miles west of Cambridge, largely concealed from the main A45 a few hundred yards away as it lies in a gentle valley in the heavy clay plateau of West Cambridgeshire, is the little village of Hardwick. It is typical of villages in eastern England, with a mixture of attractively "done up" old cottages and rather less appealing "Cambridgeshire Yellows" brick-built houses of more modern date and a flint-and-clunch church surrounded by elm trees. But just outside the village is one of the few woods for which there are records that tell of its management for over 700 years. They have been studied in detail by Dr Rackham of Cambridge University, and the account that follows is largely based on his writings. A survey made in 1251 of the estates of the Bishop of Ely, to whom the wood, along with others in the area, belonged, notes that coppicing and hurdle-making were among Hardwick's activities at that time. Other documents, now preserved at Pembroke College, Cambridge, tell of the management of the wood from 1340 onwards. Unfortunately in a number of ways this was atypical; its area was only about 21½ acres (8ha), in 1251, (this is the only definite information on its size in the Middle Ages), and instead of small numbers of the standards being felled or lopped regularly, over 500 oaks were taken for use on the Bishop's estates elsewhere in the late fourteenth century. This is likely to have involved the clear-felling of much of the wood, and it seems that it was 70 years before the large oaks were again cut.

The annual cuts of coppice also varied; 8½ acres (3.44ha) were cut in one year, although sometimes nothing was taken for several seasons. The average annual sale of timber in the fourteenth century was about 3½ acres (1.42ha), but these may not have included coppice cut by villagers who had common rights in the wood. The average rotation (the period that elapsed between the cutting of an area of coppice and its recutting) was probably between 4 and 7 years.

In 1587 the villages took legal action against Sir Francis Hynde of Madingley; they claimed he had "cutt down spoyled and Carryed away the most parte of the . . . wood" illegally. The commoners' rights were eventually set out as follows: the wood was to be coppiced in accordance with a 7 year rotation, each of 14 villagers having 1/8 acre each year, the "staddles" or standards being reserved for the Lord of the Manor. The settlement gave the the commoners the right to cut most of the wood, but it seems that small amounts of standard timber and coppice were sold. Coppice right holders were compensated on the enclosure of the village in 1837.

Hardwick Wood also differs from other woodlands in the area in that it consists only of standards and small coppice (mainly hazel). This may explain the apparent conflict with evidence (from tree-stump ring-counts and written sources) from Buff, Hayley, Gamblingay and other woods not far distant, which suggests cutting of ash and maple at intervals of 12, 13, 14, 17 or 18 years. Or it may be that observations referring to the declining years of coppicing in the nineteenth and early twentieth century are not typical, for the practice continues today in Monks Park Wood, Bradfield, Suffolk on a 7 to 10 year cycle, the poles being used, amongst other

MONKS' WOOD, near SAWTRY, Huntingdonshire.
*Valuable UNDERWOOD, OAK SAPLINGS, ASH and other FAGOTS.*

MESSRS. RICHARDSON will SELL by AUCTION, on Thursday the 24th January, 1857, 17 Acres of valuable UNDERWOOD, well filled with fine Ash Poles, Hazels, and Black Thorns; a quantity of Oak Saplings, of good lengths, suitable for strong fencing.

Mr. George Taylor, residing at Sawtry, will afford parties every facility for viewing the same prior to the day of sale.

The company are requested to meet the Auctioneers at Lot 1, at the top of Stangate Hill, near to Mr. Warsop's Farm-house, at 10 o'clock.                    10th, 1857.

*Auction and Valuation Offices, Barn-hill, Stamford, Jan.*

Notice advertising the sale of underwood from Monks Wood, Huntingdonshire in the *Lincoln, Rutland and Stamford Mercury.*                    *Dr R. C. Welch, Nature Conservancy*

things, for the production of rake-heads and handles. Formerly, as well as providing fencing and fuel, coppicing must have provided "wattle", the interlacings of twigs and rods covered with clay in "wattle and daub" timber-frame buildings.

It is interesting to speculate about the possible destinations of the vast quantities of standard timber taken from the woodlands of lowland England over the centuries; in only a small number of cases is definite evidence as to its use available to the modern enquirer. In 1322 the Norman tower of the Cathedral church at Ely collapsed; apparently the disaster was not unexpected as the pillars on which the tower was built were filled with rubble instead of being solid, and the monks had discontinued using the Choir, moving to another part of the building to say their Offices. Alan de Walsingham was the Prior to whom the task of reconstruction fell. He had to solve the problem of spanning a width of 74 feet (22.5 m) at a height of 86 feet (26.2 m) from the ground. A stone vault so vast could not be constructed in the fourteenth century and so an octagonal wooden lantern was planned. The plan required eight very large oak beams, 63 feet (19.2 m) in length, about 3 feet 4 inches (1 m) wide and 12 feet 8 inches deep. Eventually, after a great deal of searching, they were obtained from woodlands at Chicksands in Bedfordshire. Interestingly, an examination of the growth-rings in these timbers shows that they are more widely spaced than in oak trees alive today, suggesting that growth was more rapid in the Middle Ages before generations of regular coppicing and

47

felling — the removal of timber that would otherwise eventually have decayed back into the ground — had depleted the soil's supplies of plant nutrients, particularly phosphorus, an element in which the wood of both ash and hazel is relatively rich.

One of the delights greeting the visitor to the woodlands in April, May or early June is the spread of flowers that forms an uneven carpet beneath the trees. Wood anemones (*Anemone nemorosa*) provide white flashes amongst the greens of the herb-layer early in the season, while later banks of bluebells (*Endymion nonscriptus*) in the clearings appear to reflect the colour of the open summer sky in their brilliance. The light yellow flowers of the primrose brighten the path through the trees in even the gloomiest weather, and there is something particularly refreshing about the smell of damp earth in combination with the sweet, apricot-like scent of these flowers on a rainy evening.

Figure 17. Wood anemone (*Anemone nemorosa*) — a common spring flower of the woodlands.
*Mrs. P. Whitehouse*

The ecology of the primrose (*Primula vulgaris*) and the closely related oxlip (*Primula elatior*), in East Anglian woodlands has been the subject of intensive study for approaching a century. The oxlip is a splendid flower; it has a drooping umbel rather like that of the more familiar cowslip, but much larger, pale flowers, resembling those of small primroses. The drooping cluster of flowers grows from a stem up to a foot (about 30 cm) high. While the primrose is quite widely distributed and is found growing on a variety of soil types, the oxlip, or to use the old country name, paigle, has a much more restricted distribution. It is found in two main areas: — a crescent, mainly in Suffolk and Essex, but just extending into Cambridgeshire, Hertfordshire and Norfolk, from near Bishop's Stortford in the south, northwards to the valley of the River Lark and east as far as Gipping; a much smaller area in west Cambridgeshire and the fringes of Bedfordshire where it appears in a small group of ancient woods — Gamblingay, Potton, Gransden, Hayley, Knapwell, Buff, Hardwick, Overhall Grove and a few more. It seems always to be found on the "Chalky Boulder Clay" — calcareous glacial till. The oxlip is thus a very local species, but where it does occur, it is usually exceedingly abundant. An estimate of the number in Knapwell Wood in 1969, based on the number of inflorescences in 304 quadrats distributed over the wood gave a figure of 545,000 in 11.43 acres (4.64 hectares).

The oxlip forms hybrids with the primrose in those woods where both species occur, and earlier this century it was suggested that the more widespread primrose was hybridising the oxlip out of existence, but this does not seem to be the case. It appears that although the ranges of the two species do overlap — hence the hybrids — they tend to be isolated from one another by subtle difference in their ecological tolerance ranges; oxlips occur in woodlands with highly calcareous soils with a high water content. In this the species appears to resemble meadowsweet (*Filipendula ulmaria*) with which it is often associated in the woodlands. Primroses do well on much drier soils and are frequently found along hedgebanks and woodland edges.

Coppicing, of course, has a profound effect on the ground flora of a wood, although the oxlip appears very resistant to disturbance. Bluebells appear after the main annual coppicing period and thus escape the worst of the trampling. The removal of much of the canopy greatly increases the amount of direct sunlight reaching the lower layers of the wood, and may result in a temporary but substantial increase in the temperatures experienced by the ground layer vegetation and the topsoil. Coppicing has been re-established over part of Hayley Wood since 1964 by the Cambridgeshire and Isle of Ely Naturalists' Trust, a 14 year rotation being planned, and this has allowed the changes brought about by the felling to be carefully studied. These changes vary considerably according to soil type, but an increase in light often allows the establishment of taller plants such as meadowsweet, the willow-herbs (*Epilobium hirsutum* and *Chamaenerion angustifolium*) and marsh thistle (*Cirsium palustre*). They form a quite thick and sometimes colourful tangle of herbs which may provide shade for the oxlips until the hazel, ash and maple grow up again. There are parallel changes in the insect fauna.

One of the reasons why coppicing was abandoned may have been the decline in the numbers of working horses in the countryside of lowland Britain, for they provide virtually the only means of removing timber from some of these very damp woods. At Hayley today the wood has to be burnt in bonfires on the spot; around the grey rings of ash groups of creeping thistles (*Cirsium arvense*) become established.

One further point about Hayley Wood is perhaps worth mentioning. The wood was formerly skirted by a railway line, built in 1863, but closed in January 1968. The investigation of the verges along the abandoned track has provided a striking demonstration of how the edges of former woods can be plotted with almost uncanny accuracy from a study of the residual woodland flora. In places parts of Hayley Wood had to be cleared when the permanent way was laid, and in these oxlips, anemones and bluebells survive well over a century later. Plants such as rest-harrow (*Ononis repens*) characterise land that was arable before the arrival of the railway, but these do not seem to have invaded the former woodland.

Figure 18. Hayley Wood, Cambridgeshire—an example of an ancient woodland area, now protected by the local naturalist's trust.
*Cambridge University Collection*

Woodlands on the Chalk differ in many respects from those on heavy clay. Many of the oakwoods represent areas where the soil was so wet that reclamation has always been difficult. In contrast, the lighter lands of east Cambridgeshire could be cultivated with the simple ploughs of Iron Age farmers. But improved methods of husbandry enabled Anglo-Saxon and Danish immigrants to colonise the heavy clay lands, and the Chalk ridges were largely abandoned, and the beech, it seems, was able to expand. Certainly the beech is a common species in the Chalk country today; it is widely planted, occurring, for example, along estate boundaries in east Cambridgeshire and adjacent parts of Suffolk. Large stands are unusual, but 12 acres (4.86 hectares) of even-aged beechwood on the Gog Magog Hills is now managed as a reserve by the local Naturalists' Trust. These beechwoods, close to a pre-Roman trackway between Cambridge and Haverhill, are interesting botanically, for they constitute one of a small number of sites in the region where an attractive orchid, the white helleborine (*Cephalanthera damasonium*), is found. The open views in these woods, which are almost clear of any undergrowth, are in marked contrast to the restricted visibility of the tangled shrub-layer of the formerly coppiced oakwoods.

In some ways one of the most interesting areas of woodland in the eastern counties is that of Staverton Park and the adjoining area known as "The Thicks" in the parishes of Eyke and Wantisden in east Suffolk. Of the numerous ancient oaks, many are pollarded, but because the age structure is relatively uneven, it is likely that the trees are the result of a long period of natural regeneration. But here and there the antler-like branches of dead oak trees point skywards from amongst the living specimens. Birch trees are growing out of the hollowed-out hearts of now moribund oaks. There are also large numbers of holly trees, which in places form such a thick canopy that the ground-layer vegetation is absent: one holly tree is 73 ft 9 in (22.5 m) high. A few of these are probably several centuries old—some have girths of over 8 ft—but a number of them are dying. There is a middle generation of hollies, rather over a century old, and, in the clearings, a number of younger saplings. Dr Peterken, in his masterly reconstruction of the history of Staverton through the use of documentary and field sources, states that the area is an example of over-mature woodland, a community in decline. There is now no regeneration of the oaks, the acorns for the most part being consumed by immense flocks of woodpigeons; those that do survive and germinate perish through lack of light. Holly seems to be extending at the expense of the oak.

There are few records of Domesday woodland in East Suffolk, but although there is no mention of any park, wood for 30 swine is recorded as belonging to the manor of Stauertuna. The exact date of the enclosure of Staverton Park (as a preserve for game) is unknown, but the Hundred Rolls of 1275 refer to a park, so the land was presumably emparked during the period between the two surveys. As mediaeval parks were usually at least partly wooded it seems possible that the wood mentioned in 1086 formed the basis of the park. It is tempting to assume that the 20 hawks recorded in the *Records of the Earldom of Bigod* as being sold at Staverton in 1268 (9 at 2d each, 11 at 1½d) were for use in the park. The area was evidently mature oakwood in 1528, when, in September of that year, Henry VIII's sister Mary and her husband the Duke of Suffolk went fox-hunting there, and ate their meal "under the oaks".

John Norden's map of the estate of Sir Michael Stanhope, dated 1600-1601, includes the earliest known map of the park, and it shows most of the area as well wooded. A 1764 reference mentions the holly and "polled oaks", but part of the park was used as pasture for sheep in the seventeenth and eighteenth centuries, so that when preliminary mapping for the Ordnance Survey took place around 1820, the area of woodland had been reduced. Later maps confirm the continuity of tree cover, so it seems reasonable to assume that for the last 900 years woodland has existed over part of Staverton Park. It has already been shown how the great variety of corticolous lichens found at Staverton confirm the antiquity of the woodland, but there is one further piece of field evidence that merits consideration. On sandy soils, as in the Suffolk Sandlings, the removal of woodland leads to the establishment of heath, and the drastic leaching of the soil. Iron compounds, humus and other chemicals are removed from the upper layers of the soil (the A horizon) and redeposited lower down (in the B horizon). The soil so-formed is known as a Podsol. This process does not seem to have occurred anywhere beneath the Staverton woodland and so it is quite possible that woodland cover has been continuous.

Figure 19. The Staverton Park area in 1600. The forested area is recognisably similar in outline to the area wooded today. The intermingling of parkland, woodland, arable and sheepwalk (heath) is clearly seen. The map is of part of the estate of Sir Michael Stanhope, surveyed by John Norton.
*Reproduced by permission of the Archivist of the Ipswich and East Suffolk Record Office*

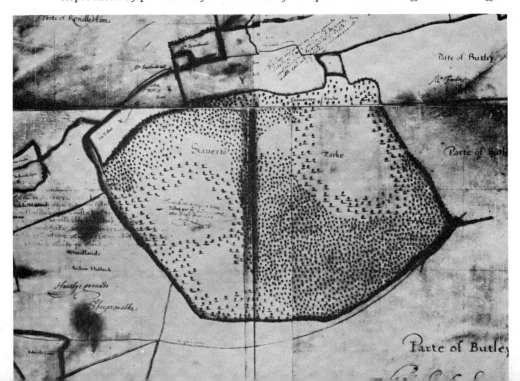

Dr Peterken writes:

"The Staverton woods are the only site where an approach to the potential natural vegetation of the Sandlings can be seen . . . Staverton Park is one of the few places in which the natural decline of a native woodland and its subsequent development can be studied. The hollies in the centre of the Thicks comprise a complete size range, supposedly the condition of primaeval woodland."

He also comments:

"In the Thicks at least dead and fallen timber lies where it falls, and a balance is developing between death and decay on one hand and regeneration and growth on the other . . . Thus although the wooods are semi-natural in common with much British woodland, the Thicks probably approaches closer to the natural condition than most other woods in lowland Britain."

There have long been other wooded parks in east Suffolk, and White's *Directory of Suffolk* for 1855 records that Rendlesham and Theberton Hall had substantial areas of timber, much of it kept to provide cover for game, but White also records that 1000 large oak trees were cut down in 1842 and sold for £8,000. But while much woodland was being felled in the eighteenth and nineteenth centuries, some efforts were being made at reafforestation, particularly in heathland areas. H. Raynbird, in his *Agriculture of Suffolk,* in 1849, encouraged the planting of windbreaks for protection, and maps made at this time show small plantations forming windbreaks around farm buildings. Most of these plantations were conifers, larch and pine being frequently used; the isolated row of stark Scots pine trees, standing out from the bracken of the surrounding heathland remains a typical feature of the East Anglian scene, both in the Suffolk Sandlings and to an even greater extent in Breckland in west Suffolk and Norfolk.

Figure 20. Windbreak of Scots pine (*Pinus sylvestris*), Norfolk.     *P. H. Armstrong*

Scots pine (*Pinus sylvestris*) was also the species favoured by the Forestry Commission in both Breckland and the Suffolk Sandlings when, in the early 1920s, a period of serious agricultural depression, they bought up large areas of uncultivated light land for tree planting. More recently there has been a shift away from Scots pine towards Corsican pine (*Pinus nigra*), which matures more rapidly and is substantially more productive under East Anglian conditions. Small areas of other conifers such as Douglas fir (*Pseudotsuga taxifolia*) have also been planted in both Breckland and the Sandlings. Broadleaved species, such as oak, beech and poplar are also used, particularly for amenity purposes along roads to relieve the relative drabness of the dark conifer plantations. There may well be other advantages in the introduction of some variety into what would otherwise be virtually single-species communities: the spread of fire and insect pests is probably reduced.

Aldewood Forest (the name given to the Forestry Commission's holdings in the Suffolk Sandlings) and Thetford Forest (the Breckland area) are the largest of the Commission's woodlands in East Anglia, although there are small areas on the light soils that stretch inland from Cromer across north Norfolk—Wesum and Lynn Forest. Thetford Forest is the largest in England; 51,500 acres or 80 square miles (20,800 hectares) is under timber. Aldewood Forest has 8,964 acres (about 3,600 hectares) of woodland and the north Norfolk forests contain another 8,000 acres or so between them. The conifer plantations—rows of trees spaced with military exactness—are divided into blocks with an average area of about 25 acres by broad rides for access and fire prevention. These rides make attractive walks through the forest and add greatly to its ecological diversity.

Figure 21. Firebreak in Thetford Forest, Norfolk.
*P. H. Armstrong*

The trees mature in about 60 years, although thinning begins after 16 years. Production of timber from Thetford Forest at present is about 125,000 cubic metres per annum, but should rise to 140,000 by 1985. (A cubic metre is approximately one ton.) But while the growing of timber has always been the principal task of the Forestry Commission, in recent years there has been a shift in emphasis and now some importance is attached to the provision of recreational facilities and forest trails and picnic areas have been laid out in all the Commission's main forests in the region. Education is also regarded as an important aspect of a state forest service's responsibilities, and large numbers of children and young persons are instructed at an impressive interpretative centre at Santon Downham, the Forestry Commission village in the heart of Thetford Forest. Just outside this village is a nursery, now highly mechanised, where young trees are raised. The technique of planting is to plough single furrows at regular intervals, and to notch the young trees into the bottom of these.

Figure 22. Rendlesham Heath, Suffolk, four years after the planting of conifers by the Forestry Commission (1923).                                                    *Forestry Commission*

Figure 23. Rendlesham Heath: conifer plantations nearly forty years old (1957).   *Forestry Commission*

An interesting, (and intensively studied) series of ecological changes follows the planting of an area of heathland with young conifer trees. There are few changes in the first five years or so, but as the pines overtop the original vegetation the heathland species are phased out. Some of the attractive heathland bird species are amongst the first to disappear, for example the stonechat (*Saxicola torquata*) — the male is splendidly distinctive with a jet black head and chestnut front — and the red-backed shrike (*Lanius collurio*), an interesting little predator which impales the insects, young birds and lizards that form its prey on thorns, have both been displaced from much of Breckland. Others, such as the nightjar (*Caprimulgus europaeus*) have, locally at least, adapted to a minor extent to forest life, nesting in the rides of some of the plantations. A heathland butterfly, the grayling (*Eumenis semele*), is sometimes to be seen flying strongly along the broader forest rides. It is remarkably camouflaged when it closes its wings; the broken pattern of buff and grey renders the insect almost invisible against the lichen and withered bracken fragments that cover the heathland soil. Amongst the heathland plants, heather, bell-heather and gorse are amongst the species that survive longest in the plantations.

A mature conifer plantation is in some respects a monotonous community, because of the thick mat of waxy needles and the dense shade few plants grow in the forest, and in any case, in a well-managed woodland the undergrowth and dead branches are removed. Birds are few; frequently the silence in the dim depths of the stands of pine trees, where rows of trunks stretch away into the distance in an almost depressing monotony is almost frightening. Small parties of marsh, coal and willow tits "chick" and "chai" and "tsee" their way about the forest and occasionally a flashing of black, white and pink accompanied by a raucous scolding "skaark" informs the visitor that he has disturbed a jay feeding beside a forest track.

Thetford Forest is a stronghold of the red squirrel (*Sciurus vulgaris*) but the American grey (*S. carolinensis*) has been advancing northwards and eastwards across East Anglia since the 1940s and is now found in the southern parts of some of the Breckland forests. The latter species is a serious pest, damaging young saplings by stripping the bark. Four species of deer occur in Thetford Forest—the red, fallow, roe, and a recent arrival (1968) the muntjac. There are substantial herds of fallow deer in Aldewood forest, and in fact in many of the larger wooded areas of the eastern counties. Although the sight of a herd of deer, or even the discovery of their rather delicate hoof-prints in damp soil, adds greatly to the interest of a woodland hike, deer also damage young trees. A balance must be struck between wildlife and forest conservation and numbers have to be controlled.

The very acid mat-like layer of needles that covers the floor of the plantation forms a most inhospitable environment for micro-organisms and insects. Fungi, therefore, are an important component of conifer woodland communities; most are saprophytes, living off dead tissues and so assisting in the decomposition of the organic matter. A stroll through almost any plantation in late summer or autumn will almost certainly provide examples of a dozen or more species of "toadstool". Quite common are the "bun fungi" (*Boletus*) which have a sponge-like underside and a brown or purplish cap; several species are edible. On stumps one may find clusters of the yellow *Gymnopilus junonius* and *Armillaria mellea,* the honey fungus. Another fungus that grows on stumps and trunks of conifers is *Fomes annosus,* a "bracket fungus" that has a hard brown resinous crust on its upperside. In plantations this organism is responsible for serious damage to conifers, particularly where they are replanted on land that has previously been clear felled or in stands where thinning has taken place, leaving stumps. The fungus enters the stump of a felled tree, growing downwards into the roots and thence to living trees nearby in which it causes a disease known as "heartrot". For some time chemical control of this pest was attempted, the stumps of Scots pine and spruce being treated with creosote, but more recently research by the Forestry Commission in Thetford Forest has resulted in the development of a type of biological control. The stumps are now treated with the spores of another fungus, *Peniophora gigantea* which keeps out *Fomes* but is not itself a tree-killer. This method of control is now used in many parts of the world. It represents one of the significant achievements of East Anglian forestry and woodland management.

# CHAPTER FOUR

# Field and Hedgerow

"Unkempt about those hedges blows
An unofficial English rose"

Rupert Brooke.
*The Old Vicarage, Grantchester*

MUCH OF the charm of any stretch of the English countyside may be attributed
to the evidence of harmonious relationships between man's activities and the
natural environment, and one of the ways in which the individuality of a region may
assert itself is the manner in which farms, fields and hedgerows blend into the
scenery. It is almost impossible to imagine eastern England without its network of
hawthorn hedges, just as it is difficult to envisage the Cotswolds or the Pennines
without the pattern of dry-stone walls that cover them.

The hedgerows of East Anglia present a paradox, for while many of the field
boundaries in the region are surprisingly young — less than two centuries old — there
are a few elements within this network that are of very great antiquity. Some
hedgebanks are well over a thousand years old and a few of these are those of estate
boundaries mentioned in Anglo-Saxon charters of the eighth, ninth and tenth
centuries. Along the boundary between the old counties of Huntingdonshire and
Northamptonshire is just such a hedge. There is a bend in the hedgerow (and in the
path that now runs along it) near a farm called Flittermere Lodge (Great Gidding
Parish). *Flittermere* is said to mean "disputed boundary" in Anglo-Saxon, so it may
be that the victors in some long-forgotten argument about estate boundaries hedged
about the ground they had won! Interestingly this hedgebank contains 12 species of
shrub; this is significant because Dr Max Hooper, who has done most to work out a
method for the study of the hedgerows of lowland England, is of the opinion that
the diversity of the shrub flora of a hedge can give valuable clues as to its age.
Briefly, in a typical 30 yard stretch of hedgerow, one may expect to find one shrub
species for every century the hedge has existed.

This shrub-counting method of dating hedges is an approximate one and considerable variations in the rate of colonisation exist, particularly in regard to soil-
type. Probably the most satisfactory application of the technique is to correlate the
species diversity with hedgerow age for a particular locality using documents and
old maps that show field boundaries and then attempting to date boundaries for

which no records exist in the same area. In the study of hedgerows, as with woodlands, therefore, work on maps and archive material must proceed together with the investigation of the hedges and their natural history in the field.

Parts of Norfolk and Suffolk were already divided into fields in early mediaeval times. In documents relating to the lands owned by a nunnery at Flixton-by-Bungay and dated 1306, 150 acres were noted as being enclosed and only 50 unenclosed. It has even been suggested that some of Suffolk's enclosures are prehistoric in origin. In one Huntingdonshire parish five miles (8km) of hedge were planted in 1364 by special licence from Edward III, and there were in fact a number of enclosures following the Black Death in 1349. There were labour shortages and sometimes land was put down to grass so that a single shepherd might replace a number of ploughmen and labourers — the wool trade of mediaeval East Anglia was beginning to expand.

By the time of Elizabeth I piecemeal enclosure, sometimes surreptitiously undertaken, was an established part of the rural tradition; often it was small closes near the village that were enclosed — it was obviously an advantage for a farmer to be able to make use of the manure from his stock on his own lands.

Yet although certain types of enclosure were made legal by a statute of 1235

Figure 24. Ridge and furrow in fields at Croxton, Cambridgeshire.   *Cambridge University Collection*

and it was possible for a landowner to obtain a licence to enclose from the reigning sovereign, this procedure was certainly not actively encouraged. Indeed there were no fewer that eleven statutes between 1489 and 1629 prohibiting unauthorised enclosure. There were also a number of Inquisitions aimed at ensuring that the provisions of the Acts were carried out. Thus it was that until a little over 200 years ago large areas remained as open fields. Charles Vancouver, in his *General View of the Agriculture of the County of Cambridge* in 1794 estimated that of the 147,000 acres of arable land in the county all but 15,000 acres (6,070 ha) lay in open fields. These arable fields were divided into strips or "furlongs" and each villager had a number of strips scattered about the manor, the idea being that each would have a fair share of good and poorer land. The strips were arranged up and down hill, partly for drainage, but also for ease of cultivation by the simple ploughs that could not turn the slice against anything but the very gentlest of gradients. This method of ploughing resulted in the building up of parallel ridges, separated by shallow furrows. Good examples of ridge-and-furrow survive at Croxton and in Wimpole Park in Cambridgeshire.

A modified form of strip-cultivation survives at Soham in Cambridgeshire and the Isle of Axholme in Lincolnshire, and vestiges of it persisted in a number of parishes in east Suffolk well into last century. The Tithe maps (described below) frequently carry the designation "common field" or "common field in parts" — the latter perhaps indicating holdings in the process of reorganisation. They also serve to show the diminutive nature of some of these holdings — an area of less than one rood was not uncommon. In trying to decipher some of these minute properties on a Tithe map, one can sense something of the difficulties and frustrations that must have been experienced by those who had to work and administer them. The map for Eyke parish, for example, made in 1846, shows a riverside plot of a few acres divided into 18 separate holdings, with several different owners and no fewer than eight occupiers. Some consolidation and exchange seems to have been taking place, as some of the larger holdings are of irregular shape. Again, the variation in the size of the strips (6 perches to 1½ acres) in the area known as The Fieldings on the Snape Map (fig. 25) tells a similar story.

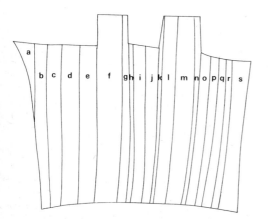

Figure 25. Strip holdings in the Fieldings, Snape, Suff in the 1840s (from Tithe Apportionment documents). T strips were held as follows: a,c,e,h,i,n,p,q — owned Alfred Barrett, occupied by Herbert Hambling; b,f,o, owned and occupied by John Hambling; d,g,m,s — ow by Page Wood, Esq., occupied by Robert French; j,k, owned by Richard Vyse, Esq., and William Hawes, Es occupied by Barry Thomas. Something of the difficulty administering a mosaic of tiny strip holdings can be se

5 chains

Many of the earlier enclosures were, in fact, "by agreement", i.e. by private negotiation between the owners of the land. When most of the land was shared by two or three owners few difficulties arose, but when a large number of interests were involved the matter might only be brought to a conclusion when considerable pressure had been exerted on one or more of the parties. In order to avoid the arrangements being challenged at some later time, perhaps by successors of the original parties to the agreement, the device of a "collusive legal action" was sometimes employed to ensure that the details of the new scheme were recorded formally. After the general outline of the reorganisation had been settled, one proprietor would fabricate some trivial claim against the remainder. He might ostensibly maintain that under the new régime a road crossed his holding, and that he should receive another half acre of land in compensation. The Enclosure would be challenged in the courts, a settlement arrived at and the final agreement enrolled in Chancery. It would then have the authority of a decided legal case.

But increasingly, in the eighteenth century landowners resorted to the Act of Parliament as an instrument of enclosure. Although expensive, it had many advantages over the older system of agreement. It permitted all the open fields in a village, together with any suitable common or waste land, to be enclosed at one and the same time. It also enabled the owners of the greater part of the land to override the objections of the smaller proprietors who might be opposed to the change. And an Act of Parliament had a legal sanctity not enjoyed by a simple agreement, for eventually queries were apt to be raised concerning the validity of any agreement finalised by the expedient of the collusive action described above.

The procedure was as follows. A group of landowners, representing at least a third of the area of the village and usually including the Lord of the manor would petition Parliament. In due course a Bill would be introduced into the House of Commons and referred to a committee constituted to receive petitions against the Bill. It would be returned to the House, passed and sent to the Lords, in due course receiving the Royal Assent.

The Bill named Commissioners, generally three in number and usually lawyers, who undertook a survey of the common lands involved and proceeded to extinguish common rights and re-allocate the land amongst the Bill's promoters and the common right holders.

Those who petitioned for enclosure had several related objectives in view. Undoubtedly they sought primarily to render farms more efficient by enlarging them, making them more compact and easier to work. Many farmers were keen to experiment with new crops, such as potatoes, turnips and some of the new varieties of grasses that had been introduced from the continent and elsewhere in the seventeenth century, and to employ some of the other new husbandry techniques being developed by Townsend and Tull, for example the "Norfolk Four Course" rotation. Enclosure also brought administrative efficiency and convenience to the village through the reorganisation of the multitudes of tiny holdings and closes. Finally there were, amongst the gentry, politicians who foresaw opposition from the independent commoner and discerned in the Enclosure movement an opportunity to consolidate their position by appropriating the greater portion of the land.

This last point has given rise to controversy. It has been argued that the Enclosure Acts were a gigantic fraud perpetrated with the purpose of securing a quick return from cheaply acquired land at the expense of the small farmer and cottager. Certainly in many cases the gentry decided the broad pattern of the redistribution of the land amongst themselves before ever the Bill came before the Committee. Amongst the documents in the Parish Chest of one of the Cambridgeshire villages the writer found sheaves of correspondence revealing the wrangling that had gone on for years before the Enclosure Award was made. The Vicar, the Lord of the Manor and the authorities of one or two of the Cambridge Colleges with interests in the village were all involved. The letter below, addressed to the Vicar from one of his advisers is typical:

Lombard St.

Jan. 10 1803

Dear H,

I thought that we had been going swimmingly on — but Old R. who (I understand signed the Bill) did not deliver his Consent yesterday, and *today* is determined to put a stop to all further proceedings unless the whole of those 7 acres which lie between his garden and M's enclosure be left to him, excepting such roads as the Commissioners think necessary. T. talked something about a Piece of waste Ground between the Vicarage premises and M's Farm which might be given to you instead, but I know of none of either Quality of Quantity such as answer the purpose. I have recommended that a specific Proposal be transmitted to you and the College as I cannot undertake for the consent of either you or them. If you know the waste I refer to, draw a little plan of it, state as nearly as you can the quantity, the condition and the fitness for cultivation and let me have your answer by return of post — But you must see the master upon it.

Yours very sincerely,       T. J.

P.S. Is there not a large pond upon this waste and would it not require much extra labour to bring it into cultivation for pasture and meadow?

It seems from the Enclosure Award for the village that Old R got his seven acres! In fact the better part of the lands of the village were divided amongst the Vicar, R, T and two of the Cambridge Colleges!

The Enclosure Map for a parish, often an impressive piece of cartography up to 6 feet long, showing the new pattern of field boundaries resulting from the changes, is often quite similar to the network of hawthorn hedges that one sees today. The Award that accompanies the Map (both are usually held by the local record office) shows the area of each parcel of land and its owners.

Enclosure by Act of Parliament was most important between 1750 and 1850. Thus, to take some Cambridgeshire examples, Knapwell was enclosed in 1775, Trumpington in 1804 and Cottenham in 1847.

Another set of documents useful in the study of the evolution of the pattern of field boundaries in a parish are those relating to the Commutation of tithes following the *Tithe Commutation Act* of 1836. For centuries farmers had been required to deliver one tenth of their produce to the Tithe-Holder, usually the church. Needless to say many objected to this, especially the giving away of a proportion of any increase in yield their endeavours were able to secure. Some tithe-payers devoted considerable enterprise to devising schemes to annoy or cheat the tithe-owners. There is a story that a farmer informed the parson that he was going to pull his turnips and when the parson's man arrived at the field with a cart, the farmer pulled out just ten roots and gave one to the carter, announcing that he would let his master know in due course when more were to be taken!

There were countless anomalies; some produce was titheable, some was not; there were variations in custom from place to place. Lord Rendlesham was impropriator of the tithes on his own land at Kesgrave in Suffolk and in the same part of the country a holding of 23 acres (93 ha) at Benacre was exempt from tithes because it was dissolved monastic land. The situation was clearly absurd and the 1836 Act provided for Assistant Commissioners to assess the value of the tithes in money terms so that it could be commuted to a money payment. A *Tithe Map* was prepared for each parish in which there was titheable land, showing the various holdings and their crops, and a dossier of documents relating to the tithes and their commutation was also prepared, the *Tithe File*. These materials now provide a valuable source of material for studies of the land-use pattern of the early nineteenth century, especially the Tithe Maps and the attached *Apportionments*. All these records are held by the Public Record Office, although in many cases a second copy is deposited in the local record or archive office.

From about 1872 onwards the Six Inch sheets of the Ordnance Survey are available, and for the last three decades or so there may be air photo coverage. Thus the evolving pattern of field boundaries for some parts of East Anglia can be traced through some two or three centuries. The Cambridge colleges have long had substantial holdings in many East Anglian parishes and have good collections of documents relating to these. For these farms, and occasionally for others, maps and plans can sometimes be found covering an even longer period.

There are, of course, difficulties in the dating of hedgerows even when good documentation is possible. For example, an Enclosure Award of a certain date might specify that the boundaries of each allotment were to be " hedged about" within a year of the award, and thus these hedges can be dated with complete accuracy. But the subdivision of any one allotment might have been made as and when the landowner thought fit; internal hedgerows may be of rather late date. In many cases appropriate maps and documents do not exist and the shrub-counting technique may be the only method of dating available.

A truly ancient hedge — an old manorial boundary or one mentioned in tenth century Anglo-Saxon charters — may have accumulated some dozen shrub species. Species typical of older hedges are the Midland hawthorn (*Crataegus oxycanthoides*) field maple (*Acer campestre*) and spindle-tree (*Euonymus europaeus*). A hedge dating from Elizabethan times will perhaps contain four or five species. The farmhouse at Rookery Farm, Monewden, Suffolk was built in 1593, on land quite recently cleared of forest. In May 1656 one Nathaniel Fuller made a map of the farm, which was divided into about a dozen fields with names such as Horse Pightle (enclosure), Newland Close (significant name?), Stack Close and Church Meadow. The pattern of field boundaries has survived almost unaltered from the time when Nathaniel undertook his survey, and probably from when the land for the farm was laid out, down to the 1970s, and several of the hedges contain five species of shrubs. Some of the pasture land enclosed by these ancient living hedges is extremely interesting ecologically. The damp, sandy clay loam soil has probably never been ploughed, the meadows having been cut for hay for centuries. The plants growing amongst the grasses include the green-winged orchis (*Orchis morio*), wild daffodil (*Narcissus pseudonarcissus*), yellow-raffle (*rhinanthus minor*) and the fritillary or snake's head (*Fritillaria meleagris*). Grasslands which have been ploughed or reseeded from time to time have a much less colourful and interesting flora.

Hawthorn was the species favoured by many of the enclosing landlords as it grew rapidly on most types of soil and quickly formed an efficient barrier to stock. Hedges that date from the Enclosure Acts of last century therefore contain hawthorn and at most one other species; on heavy clay soils it is sometimes partnered by blackthorn (*Prunus spinosa*), on Chalk privet (*Ligustrum vulgare*) may occur and elder (*Sambucus nigra*) may accompany hawthorn on light sandy soils. Other species of shrub have been planted in hedgerows locally — beech is used on some large estates in Norfolk and elm is not uncommon in east Suffolk.

In 1962 it was estimated that there were 616,000 miles (about a million km) of hedge in Great Britain. If one assumes that the average hedge is about two yards (1.83m) wide, then hedges at that time covered 448,000 acres (181,300 ha). The hedgerow, bright with pale pink wild roses and the tiny purple and yellow flowers of woody nightshade (*Solanum dulcamara*) in early summer and with the red berries, haws and rosehips that follow in the autumn is an important component of the English landscape and tradition. Yet the hedgerow habitat has received relatively little scientific study.

It is a complex community. Frequently a drainage ditch runs parallel to the hedge itself and the earth dug from it may be piled up on the other side of the ditch, on the hedge side or on both sides of it. Depending on the orientation of the boundary one side of the hedge may be almost permanently in shade. There may thus be subtle variations in microclimate (temperature, sunlight, humidity and so forth), soil character and drainage conditions within a very short distance, and many dozens of plant species may grow within a few feet of one another, each having slightly different environmental requirements. Rushes (*Juncus*) may become established in the ditch if it is not regularly cleaned out; knapweed, foxgloves and primroses may provide splashes of colour in the hedgebank and bindweed (*Convolvulus arvensis*) and old man's beard (*Clematis vitalba*) climb in amongst the shrubs and small trees.

A great range of creatures of all sizes are dependent on hedgerows for food and shelter. Probably about 60 species of British moth caterpillars feed on hawthorn; this includes 5 species of leaf-miners (caterpillars that feed on the interior tissues of the leaves, the outer skins being left intact) as well as two berry-eaters that feed upon no other plant. The larvae of the peacock butterfly (*Nymphalis io*) feed on the nettles growing in clumps along the hedgebank, the adult insects taking nectar from the hedgerow flowers. There are a number of species of insects that spend part of their life cycle in hedgerows and the remainder in the nearby fields, the juxtaposition of the two habitats being important for their survival. Many studies have confirmed that the great majority of the 50 or so bird species of English farmland are dependent on hedgerows for part of their food, for nesting sites or for both—yellowhammers, linnets, song thrushes, blackbirds and whitethroats all nest in hedges. A figure of one bird's nest per 25 yards of hedge in East Anglia is probably not far from the truth. The lapwing and the skylark are amongst the few species that breed in open farmland. In winter haws form a substantial proportion of the food of migrants such as the fieldfare and redwing. The sight of flocks of these thrushlike visitors from northern Europe assembled to feed on a well-laden hawthorn hedge frequently enlivens an otherwise uneventful winter stroll. The network of hedges also serves to link the small woods and copses scattered over the countryside, enabling animals to move between them.

John Clare wrote:
> "And birds and trees and flowers without a name
> All sighed when lawless law's enclosure came."

He was lamenting the disappearance of common and waste-land following the implementation of the Enclosure Acts. He perhaps did not appreciate the extent to which the hedgerows would provide a refuge for many species displaced from these other habitats, and would certainly have been disturbed by the current rate of hedgerow destruction. In 1968 the Nature Conservancy undertook a survey of England's hedges and estimated that they were disappearing at the rate of 7,000 —

14,000 miles (approx. 11,300—22,600lm) per annum, the rate of removal being highest in the arable areas of eastern England. The table below, the work of Dr Max Hooper at the Conservancy's Experimental Station at Monks Wood, gives an indication of the changes which have occurred in the total length of hedgerow in an area in three parishes in the former county of Huntingdonshire.

Length of hedge on 4,000 acres (about 1,600 ha) in the parishes of Buckworth, Barham and Woolley and Leighton Bromswold, near Huntingdon.

| Date | Length of hedge | | Comment |
|------|------|------|---------|
| Before | miles | km | |
| 1364 | 20 | 32 | Manorial boundary |
| 1364 | 25 | 40 | Enclosure for deer park and pasture by licence from Edward III |
| 1500 | 28 | 45 | Private enclosure |
| 1550 | 32 | 51 | Private enclosure |
| 1680 | 46 | 74 | Private enclosure |
| 1780 | 58 | 93 | Enclosure Act for one manor; whole area now enclosed |
| 1850 | 76 | 122 | Evidence from Tithe maps for subdivision of former large enclosures |
| 1946 | 70.8 | 112 | Removal of hedgerows with increasing mechanisation of arable farming |
| 1963 | 46 | 74 | |
| 1965 | 20.8 | 34 | |

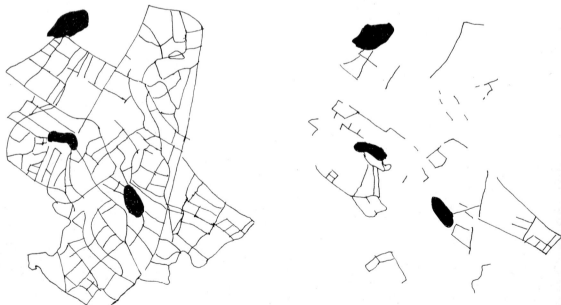

Figure 26. Left: the hedges in a group of three parishes in Huntingdonshire in 1946, from aerial photographs. Right: the hedges in the same area in 1965.

*Reproduced by kind permission of Dr Max Hooper*

The pattern is clear and is typical of much of lowland England; the length of hedgerows reached a peak in the later part of the nineteenth century following the Enclosures. In the period 1946-65 the rate of hedgerow loss was 0.53 miles/100 acres.

In another study, undertaken at the University of East Anglia, air photographs of Norfolk taken by the Royal Air Force in 1946 and 1947 were compared with photos taken during an aerial survey in 1969-70. Information on field boundaries — the removal of hedges and the combination of small fields to make larger enclosures and so on—was then transferred to large scale Ordnance Survey maps. The boundaries were later traced from these maps using a machine called an electronic line follower. A computer was then programmed to calculate the length of hedgerow removed and the average area of fields before and after removal. The percentage of boundary removed was about 50% of the 1946 length for the county of Norfolk as a whole although it was as low as 6½% in areas such as the Good Sands region of north Norfolk where fields were already large. A total of about 8,000 miles of hedge were removed in Norfolk in the 24 year period.

It has been calculated that the ideal size and shape for a field from the point of view of a farmer wishing to use modern agricultural machinery to its optimum extent, is a square enclosure of 50 acres (20.2 ha). The time lost in turning and stopping combines and other large implements is reduced and wasteful overlap in the spreading of seed, lime and fertilisers is prevented. Also, additional cultivable farmland can be reclaimed at the rate of about one acre for each mile of hedge removed. It is further pointed out that frost may linger along the edges of fields where tall hedges cast their shadows and that hedgerows may harbour seed-eating birds and other pests which may consume part of the crop. Hedges are also costly to maintain; in 1965 it was calculated that £1,500 per annum would be saved by the grubbing up of 48 miles (75 km) of hedges on a 2,000 acre (c. 800 ha) holding.

But powerful arguments can be advanced against those who advocate the removal of hedgerows. Several experiments have demonstrated that moisture loss from the soil is increased by the higher wind velocities blowing over farmland from which all windbreaks have been removed. Some German investigators claim that yields of cereals and other crops are considerably increased by the existence of hedgerows. Another argument is that they provide refuges for predators that feed on the insect pests of the nearby farmland, and in some areas they have been proved to reduce soil erosion. They provide cover and nesting sites for partridges and so may allow a crop of game to be taken from a farm as well as one of barley. Rare plants sometimes survive in hedges where the woodland with which they were formerly associated has disappeared or been reduced. They also have great aesthetic appeal: there are many who rejoice in the slightly irregular pattern of hedgerows that still covers much of the subdued landscape of eastern England and the outlines of the elm trees rising from the hedges are silhouetted against the sky.

The dilemma is a complex one, and only further research can resolve the problem. Detailed studies of the hedgerow community, emphasising both economic and ecological aspects of the problem are continuing at Monks Wood Experimental Station near Huntingdon and the Arthur Rickwood Experimental Husbandry Farm at Mepal near Ely. There has in fact been a slight decline in hedgerow removal since 1966, partly because in some areas there were few hedges left to be taken out. The Ministry of Agriculture formerly gave a subsidy for removing hedges, but this policy was discontinued in 1972.

The traditional method of managing hedges involves a technique known as "pleaching" or "plashing". The tools required for this are a felling axe, a billhook and a slasher — the shapes of the billhook and the slasher vary considerably from one area to another. As much as possible of the rough undergrowth is cut away and many of the actual hedge growths are also removed. Those that remain are half severed with the billhook close to the base and bent over at an angle of 45° to the ground, sometimes being intertwined with stakes driven into the hedge. The process varies in detail from place to place; in some parts of eastern England no stakes are used but a few long, slender shoots are left as "hethers" or binders and are wound in and out of the "laid" hedge to bind it together and render it stockproof. However, this work is skilled and cost in labour of laying the hedges on a large farm is considerable. Increasingly, where boundaries remain, farmers are resorting to another method of hedge management. This consists of cutting the hedge right down to within a few inches of the soil and then allowing it to grow again. Hawthorn is the only hedge shrub species which will survive this drastic treatment. Although the protection and ecological diversity of the hedgerow is lost, for a time at least, the method allows the cultivation of the soil to the very margins of an enclosure.

Figure 27. A Cambridgeshire hedgerow cut almost to ground level.                    *P. H. Armstrong*

Figure 28. A well-laid Cambridgeshire hedge.                    *P. H. Armstrong*

The importance and attractiveness of the hedgerow timber element in the East Anglian landscape has already been commented upon. Oak, elm and ash are the three commonest species and it is these trees growing along eighteenth century and earlier boundaries which give an exaggerated impression to the traveller of the extent that the countryside of parts of south Cambridgeshire or Norfolk, for example, are wooded. Oak is a particularly common hedgerow tree in Norfolk, elm being more frequent in the hedges of Cambridgeshire and Suffolk.

"Elmwood burns like churchyard mould" runs an old country rhyme, for the elm provides a poor firewood, a fuel that splutters in the grate without giving out much heat. But the elm tree makes up for this deficiency: who can fail to feel something of the exhilaration of early summer when he sees the elms along the field boundaries of eastern England standing upright, appearing to pull their green cloaks around them to give the illusion of extra height against a vivid blue sky? And can anyone fail to be impressed by the way in which the trees appear, a delicate intermediate shade between yellow and orange, as luminous cascades of falling leaves in late October? Even when bare branches reach towards sombre skies as one takes a short walk along any hedgerow on a windy winter day one may be just a little awed by the way in which the boughs of elm trees creak and groan in a manner somehow different from that of any other species of tree. Elms are also important to wildlife; many species of birds nest in the holes that frequently occur in their trunks.

The English elms (there are several closely related species found in the eastern counties) with their irregularly ridged bark and unshaven looking trunks — they are often covered with wisp-like sucker shoots — and asymmetrical serrated leaves are also part of the English literary scene: Tennyson wrote of "The moan of doves in immemorial elms".

69

Unforunately it cannot be assumed that the elm will remain an important element in East Anglia's countryside. A fungal infection of Asian origin, now called Dutch elm disease, appeared first in Britain in 1927 after having done considerable damage to trees in France and Holland during the early 1920s. It is spread by a small (¼in), reddish-brown wood-boring beetle called *Scolytus*. The insects lay their eggs in tunnels beneath the bark of elm trees, where the larvae live by eating the wood. Eventually the adult beetles eat their way out through the bark and depart, carrying spores of the fungus with them. The effect of the fungus is to block up the sap channels in the trees. There were severe outbreaks of the disease in Britain in 1927 and 1950, but because of the natural vigour of elm trees, these appear to have done little permanent harm. Some of the elm trees in Cambridgeshire, for example, have recovered from Dutch elm disease at least twice. However the outbreak of the infection in the 1970s seems to have been rather more destructive and was accorded a great deal of publicity. In May 1972 it was estimated that one and a half million of the 25 million or so elms in southern and eastern England were dead or dying from the disease, and many hundreds of thousands more were infected to a lesser extent and became "stag-headed". Essex, Suffolk and Hertfordshire were particularly hard hit, the incidence of the disease declining as one moved northwards. Attempts were made to control its spread by felling or lopping and burning the affected wood. Specimen trees of amenity value can be injected against infection, but the treatment costs £8 per tree and has to be repeated annually. Some natural control, such as a severe winter destroying large numbers of the beetles, may eventually prove more effective than the efforts of the foresters.

Unfortunately Dutch elm disease is not the only agency bringing death to hedgerow trees. Along roadsides and field boundaries in many parts of Norfolk, Suffolk and Cambridgeshire one sees the dead branches of many stag-headed ash and oak trees extending forlornly skywards. Many theories have been put forward to explain this unhappy state of affairs. Possible causes include the following: atmospheric pollution; damage to the roots of trees through deep ploughing too close to the trees; damage following the spread of carelessly tended autumn stubble fires to nearby hedges; accumulation of chemicals in the lower layer of the soil following several decades of leaching of agricultural fertilisers; lowering of the water table following improvements in land drainage; exposure following the removal of hedgerow cover; deliberate poisoning of trees subject to preservation orders by farmers wishing to remove trees in order to increase the size of their fields. It is to be hoped that the increasing "amenity consciousness" of the community and movements such as the "Plant a Tree in '73" campaign will encourage the planting of native species of trees and prevent the complete transformation of East Anglia into a monotonous, if productive, arable prairie.

Others types of boundaries besides hedges are met with; flint-faced walls are quite common in parts of Norfolk, Suffolk and south-east Cambridgeshire.

Figure 29. Diseased elms, Cambridgeshire.

*P. H. Armstrong*

Generally the walls are faced with well-shaped stones set in mortar, the interior being filled with rubble. Frequently these walls are topped by a course of brickwork. In the narrow strip of west Norfolk between Hunstanton and Downham Market walls are of the local carstone. Another example of the use of local material in the construction of boundaries is in the use of the produce of the marshlands and reed-beds of East Anglia to make reed-fences. They appear in the Fens, the Norfolk Broads and there used to be one in Iken churchyard in Suffolk. As one might expect, they are also common in the Netherlands. There is a thatched wall at Orwell in Cambridgeshire.

Farms and fields are nearly always entered through a wooden gate; in eastern England five horizontal cross-pieces are usual, although gates with four or six bars are met with from time to time. There is in any case wide variation in the design of gates—several dozen types may be noted in a single county. Nevertheless certain regional tendencies can be distinguished; for example a five-barred gate strengthened with two wooden Xs can be seen across the entrance to many an East Anglian farm but would be quite unusual in the north country or the west of England.

Figure 30. East Anglian five-barred gate, with the carved "jowl"—the craftsman's personal mark— adjacent to the hinge.
                                                                                    *P. H. Armstrong*

Figure 31. "Kissing" or "wishing" gate, Grantchester Meadows, Cambridgeshire.     *P. H. Armstrong*

The post to which the gate is hinged is called the "swinging post" while the other is generally referred to by farmers as the "clapping post". The upright limb of the gate at the hinge end is known as the "arr", "harr" or "artree". Sometimes a gate is seen with the harr curling over, above the main part of the gate. This allows the diagonal spar or "swape" to make a greater angle with the horizontal than it would otherwise, strengthening the whole structure. A gate of this design is also easily closed by someone on horseback; the type seems to have been commoner in the past than at present, as it is often pictured in old hunting prints.

"Kissing-gates", small gates hung in U- or V-shaped enclosures, are erected in special situations. They are more expensive than the normal five-barred gate, but have the advantage that they cannot be left open. They are thus employed on well-used rights of ways through pastures where stock is kept. There are several along the path running through the meadows close to the River Granta between Cambridge and Grantchester.

Some gates are still made by a local carpenter near the farm on which they are used, although increasingly they are being mass-produced in factories in some distant part of the country. Also gateways are having to be enlarged to take increasingly sophisticated machinery, and often an older locally made gate is replaced by a more efficient but rather characterless tubular steel structure. Changes of this kind and the removal of hedges may have advantages if British agriculture is to remain competitive, but the sight of a well laid hedge or an unusually designed, albeit rather tumbledown old gate, contribute to one's enjoyment of the countryside and are worthy of careful observation and serious attention while they remain.

# CHAPTER FIVE

# The Vanishing Heaths

"Lo! where the heath with withering brake grown o'er,
Lends the light turf that warms the neighbouring poor;
From thence a length of burning sand appears,
Where the thin harvest waves its withered ears."

George Crabbe
*The Village*

(Brake = bracken)

THERE are two areas of East Anglia where sandy heathlands were formerly widespread: the east Suffolk Sandlings and Breckland in west Suffolk and adjacent areas of Norfolk.

The term Sandland or Sandlands was used in the eighteenth century. In 1735 John Kirby described the area in these terms:

"The Sandland may be divided into the marsh, arable and heathlands. The marshland is naturally fruitful, fatting great numbers of oxen and sheep; and sometimes, when ploughed affords the greatest crops of corn of any other land in the country. That part which is arable is in some places good for tillage and produces excellent crops of all sorts of corn, and where it is in a manner barren, it is found fit for improvement by chalk rubbish, and a late discovered cragg or shell . . . the heathy part may contain about one third of the Sandlands and is used for sheep walks."

Kirby emphasises here the diversity of types of land and notes that the three categories, drained marshland, arable and heath, were integrated into a common farming system. Arthur Young, in his *General view of the Agriculture of Suffolk* included a map showing the area of sandy soils extending from Yarmouth to Ipswich, a zone about 10 miles (16 km) wide along the Suffolk coast.

The area is one of very gentle relief; few points are more than about 70 ft above sea-level; the interfluves are of sandy Pleistocene Crag material and have extremely acid soils, while in the hollows—some of them only separated from the sea by a narrow shingle ridge or spit—lie extensive tracts of wetland. George Crabbe wrote of the Sandlings landscape: "Fen, marshes, bog and heath all intervene . . .".

Heathland covers a fair proportion of the higher ground, although, because of many generations of reclamation for arable, few unbroken areas of any size remain outside the national nature reserves at Westleton Heath and Walberswick; but many of the scattered fragments of heathland that do exist make up for their small size in the variety of plant communities within them. Some heaths, especially those that have been grazed by cattle or sheep within living memory appear a blaze of yellow gorse (*Ulex europaeus*) in the early summer; as autumn approaches the brown-black patches of ling and bell-heather become tinged with purple. Even in winter the heaths appear colourful, as it is then that the stands of bracken (*Pteridium aquilinum*), withered to a mellow russet-brown, appear most attractive.

Around the Breckland towns of Mildenhall, Brandon and Thetford the low escarpment that forms the backbone of East Anglia disappears, the Chalk dipping below the surface. The resulting depression has an infilling of chalky glacial till and fluvio-glacial deposits from which much of the lime has been removed by percolating rainwater, and the sandy soils that have resulted from this have long been liable to wind-blow, erosion and sand-storms. in 1668 a storm blew sand for some five miles from Lakenheath Warren, almost overwhelming the village of Santon Downham, and obstructing navigation in the Little Ouse. A story is told of a Breckland landowner, who, when asked in which county, Norfolk or Suffolk, his property was situated, replied "Sometimes in the one, sometimes in the other; it blows backwards and forwards!" In this dry area, human settlement has been largely confined to the river valleys — those of the Little Ouse, the Nar, the Thet, the Wissey and the Lark. Between the valleys there were once broad stretches of heath, almost continuous and far more extensive than the scattered heaths of the Sandlings. There is nothing quite comparable with the variety afforded by the mosaic of land-types to be seen in the east Suffolk coastlands. But as in the coastal area, the character of the region has been much changed over the past few decades through the acquisition of large tracts of land by the Forestry Commission (see Chapter Three). Also, as in the coastal zone much of the heathland has been ploughed up; in particular Lord Iveagh on the Elveden estate has demonstrated that even the most infertile soils may be cultivated profitably if sufficient capital is available and if reclamation is undertaken on a large enough scale.

The importance of these two regions as areas for human settlement in prehistoric times has already been stressed. Such pollen evidence as there is suggests that the forests were cleared early and were replaced by an open plant community; patches of woodland, however, probably persisted into Anglo-Saxon times. Sheep seem to have grazed over East Anglia's heaths for much of the historic period; for example, flocks of 1,000 sheep are recorded in Domesday at Icklingham and Santon Downham in Breckland. Coming closer to the present, an interesting glimpse into the agricultural pattern of the mid-seventeenth century Sandlings is afforded by a series of accounts preserved in the East Suffolk Record Office, showing the management of flocks at Westwood, near Blythburgh in the years 1646-7:

| "(Sold) to Richard Sortes 2 Ewes and a lamb at | £ 1 | 10 | 0 | |
|---|---|---|---|---|
| To Sir Thomas Bomesdiston 100 lambs at 4s 4d | £26 | 0 | 0 | (sic) |
| To William Copeland 60 lambs at 3s 6d | £10 | 10 | 0 | |
| There was sett 222 lambs, which were added to the weather flock worth | £60 | 0 | 0 | |

If we accept a lambing rate of a little less than one lamb per ewe and make allowance for a small number of rams, it can be calculated that there must have been about 1000 sheep in the flock at Westwood in the summer of 1646. It is of interest that, the celebrated eighteenth century agricultural writer Arthur Young, in his desire to learn as much as possible of the advances in agriculture that were taking place in Suffolk at the time, visited Westwood Farm in 1784 and again in 1795, and wrote in detail about the husbandry techniques he found in use there. He mentions that there was a flock of 1600 sheep on the farm in 1795 and wrote:

"The dry heaths are to be profitably managed only by sheep being made the principal object, and all the tillage of the farm absolutely subservient to them."

The flock was in fact an important ecological link between the different land-types found on the typical Sandlings landed estate of the time; each had substantial areas of heathland or sheepwalk, arable land and drained marshland. The heaths provided food for the sheep in the early summer and also in winter when heather shoots protruded above the snow; the marshes were grazed throughout much of the year, but particularly in spring. The arable land was used to produce clover in the summer and turnips as winter fodder, both of these being eaten in the fields by the sheep. The flock was almost always folded on the arable part of the farm at night. A lease for Westwood of this date specified:

"Tennant to keep at least 800 sheep and to fold them at all reasonable times in the year with the usuall number of hurdles upon some part of the farm most likely to be benfited thereby, under penalty of £5 a night the flock or at least 600 thereof shall not be folded on the said part of the premises."

The *Account of the Profitts of the Ewe Flocks* at Westwood in 1646 mentioned above also includes references to the sheep being folded on the nearby ploughed land and a mention of 10s being paid for hurdle making. The sheep dung fertilized the fields, and in Arthur Young's time the soil's fertility was further improved by the nitrogen-fixing bacteria in the roots of the clover. Crops of wheat (sometimes barley) were taken from the arable land about one year in four.

The heathland, as well as providing grazing for the sheep, was also utilised as a source of bedding for stock and of brushwood for the repair of the ditches draining the lowland pastures.

The continuity of this tight integration of the sheep and arable enterprises was maintained into the nineteenth century. Between the years of 1831 and 1842 a Mr. Samuel Gross kept a diary relating to his activities on several farms in the southern

Sandlings (now preserved in the East Suffolk Record Office). This indicates that "coal-worts" (cole wort — a primitive form of kale), turnips and swedes were grown to provide a succession of foods for the flocks in the winter months. Usually, in April, when both turnips and swedes were exhausted, the sheep were put on the lowland pastures. Mr Gross also describes sending the flock to graze on nearby heaths and commons, and he also mentions collecting heather and gorse from the heathland to put down in his farmyard. Another nineteenth century observer, H. Rainbird, confirms: "Whin, fern and ling grow . . . along most of these heaths . . . Large flocks of sheep are fed on these heaths and are folded on adjoining land". Indeed, as recently as the First Land Utilisation Survey in the 1930s the pattern does not seem to have been very different; R. W. Butcher wrote in 1941:

> ". . . sheep are the mainstay of the arable farmers . . . The sheep run for the most part on the heaths and poor grassland in the summer, are folded in the green crops in the autumn and stall fed on the roots in the winter."

Sheep were also extremely important on the Breckland heaths. Recent researches by Mrs G. Crompton on the land use history of the 2,500 acres of Lakenheath Warren in Breckland, shows that probably for several centuries rights existed allowing 2,040 sheep to graze upon the warren. As in the case of the Sandlings heaths, the sheep were folded on the arable land at night and grazed over the warren by day. An eighteenth century traveller, F. Bloomfield wrote of the sheep of the Norfolk Breck that there was "no where better Mutton than this barren land affords, the Sheep being not liable to the Disease called the Rot."

Thus certainly for about nine hundred years, perhaps for much longer, the farmers of East Anglia have depended on the heathlands for their stock's summer grazing. Some of the sheepwalks at least were as carefully managed as the arable lands that they complemented. The aim was, as Arthur Young put it, to secure "a good covering of furze and ling". With this in view some of the Sandlings heaths were regularly cut and burnt.

Substantial tracts of heathland were common land and the Common Rights were jealously guarded, local regulations concerning the numbers of stock that individuals could put on the common being legally enforced. The court rolls of many manors in the heathland districts contain references to small fines being imposed for illegal grazing, and there was, for example, continuing friction between the villagers of Walberswick in east Suffolk, and the Lord of the Manor, a Sir Robert Brooke, throughout the middle years of the seventeenth century. In 1639 the dispute went as far as the Inner Star Chamber. "The matter of the rights of Commonage" was the principal point at issue. The dispute seems to have dragged on, however, for in 1642 it was alleged that the "Commons, containing above 1,400 acres, together with Fennes" had been withheld from the villagers for thirty years.

This grazing by sheep would have effectively prevented the invasion of the heaths by scrub and their eventual transformation into woodland, but there was another type of pressure that assisted in the maintenance of the open character of the heathlands—their use as rabbit warrens.

The former warrens of Breckland are well-known; there were eight on the sandy heathlands of west Suffolk and Norfolk, probably established in the second half of the thirteenth century. The establishment of a warren was originally accomplished by the grant of a Charter of Free Warren by the king; he received a substantial sum of money in return for the granting of the exclusive right to take the "beasts and fowls of warren". These were defined by the sixteenth century lawyer, Manwood, as "such as may be taken by long-winged hawks; and those are the hare, the coney (rabbit), the pheasant and none other." In 1300 the Prior of Ely is recorded as owning a warren at Lakenheath, and there is mention of a *cunicularium* at Eriswell in 1309. The warrens were of several thousand acres and in each a warren lodge was built of flint and Barnack stone in a commanding position.

Figure 32. Sixteenth century map of Methwold Warren, Norfolk.     *Public Record Office MS MPC 75*

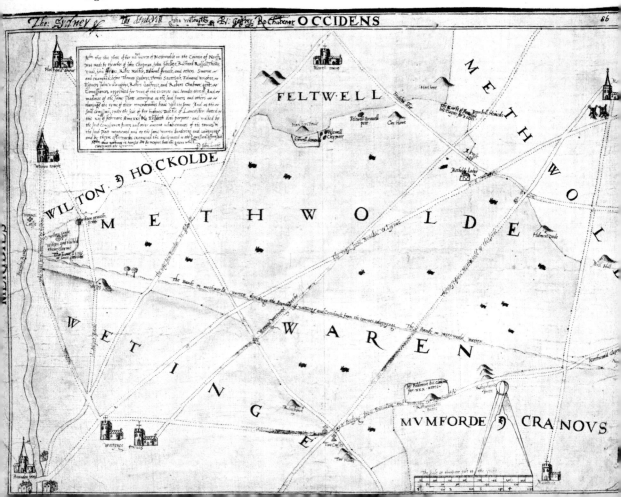

Figure 33. The Warren Lodge, Thetford Warren.                    *Forestry Commission*

They were to defend the warrens—in their hey-day they were very valuable properties—from poachers and to provide accomodation for the warrener and his labourers. The remains of lodges on Mildenhall and Thetford Warrens still stand—that at Thetford is a remarkably robust, square building dating from about the fourteenth century, now surrounded by birch scrub. At Eriswell and Methwold a few fragments of stone set into seventeenth and eighteenth century farm buildings are all that remain of the former lodges. At Lakenheath in the seventeenth century there were no fewer than three lodges on the warren, but of these nothing remains today.

During the six hundred years that the Lakenheath Warren was systematically managed, it was surrounded by turf banks; along part of the 10 miles (16km) or so of boundaries a second bank can still be seen running parallel to the main barrier. Gorse branches were placed along the top of the bank. The rabbits were taken using dogs, ferrets, nets and traps, the latter sometimes placed adjacent to holes through the inner surrounding walls. W. A. Dutt, writing in 1906 in his *Wild Life in East Anglia,* described how rabbits were caught on some warrens by means of "tipes". These tipes were circular pits eight or nine feet deep; each was covered by a delicately balanced iron door, turing on a swivel, on which food was placed. The weight of a rabbit caused the iron door to "tipe" so that the animal fell into the pitfall beneath. It is said that as many as 2,000 rabbits were caught in a single night on Thetford Warren in this manner.

In the fourteenth century 4,000 rabbits per year were sometimes taken from Brandon Warren; Arthur Young, for the same warren in 1794 quoted a catch of ten times that figure. 25,000 per annum was the estimate given by a landlord in an accusation against the tenant of Eriswell in 1776, although apparently on the basis of very little evidence. Young, writing of Suffolk warrens in 1794, regretted that it was "very difficult to gain a satisfactory knowledge of the acreable produce of the land, in this application of the soil, for the warrens are more commonly estimated than measured." He does, however, suggest that 10 per acre per year "may not be far from the fact". This figure agrees quite well with data submitted from Breckland warrens in evidence to the *House of Commons Select Committees on the Game Laws* which sat in the 1840s and 1870s. In May 1845 a Mr J. Chambers was examined by the Committee on the production of his Breckland Warren. When asked how many rabbits he took from his warren each season, he replied: "About 20,000 on the 2,000 acres: but that would be at heavy expense (in terms of hay and similar feed in winter). If they were fed only with the natural produce of the warren, there would not be more than 7 or 8 rabbits to the acre." The yield seems to have decreased in the later nineteenth and early twentieth century on some warrens in the area. At Lakenheath between 1915 and 1940 the average number of rabbits killed was 1.8 per acre.

Warrens seem to have been established in the east Suffolk Sandlings at about the same time as in Breckland. Amongst the earlier grants of free warren relating to this region is one dated February 1265 to "Richard le Scot of Dunwich, and his heirs, of the free warren in his demesne lands in Mennesmeer (Minsmere), Westleton, Middleton, Fordle, Walpole and Dunwich in Suffolk." A clear picture of the use made of the grants of free warren can be gained from ancient records now preserved in the British Museum, which state that in 1268 twelve hawks were sold at Framlingham in east Suffolk, costing 1½d each. In 1271 thirty-four hawks were sold there at 2½d each. These hawks may have been either sparrow hawks or goshawks; Reyce, in his *Breviary of Suffolk,* wrote in 1619 that "the Sparhauke and Gossehauke are found here in diverse places, oftentimes to breed butt nothing so commonly as in the former times . . . ". Traps, nets, dogs and ferrets were also used, as they were in Breckland, and alongside the references to the sale of hawks at Framlingham in 1268 is a note that two nets cost 3d.

As with certain Breckland warrens, the history of some of those in the Sandlings can be traced in some detail. Following the original grant of rights in the thirteenth century, at least one warren in east Suffolk seems to have been carefully managed for several centuries. A lease, dated 1499 now preserved in the Ipswich archives office, for "all that woreyne of coneys in Blyburgh (Blythburgh) belonging to the manor of Westwood as well within the park as without" gives an interesting glimpse of the way in which a warren was managed. The lease was to run for fifteen years and the annual rent was 14s. A number of conditions were laid down. The warrener (his name, perhaps significantly, was John Woreyn) was forbidden "to hunt any dere" in the warren; he might graze "one horse of his owne to his owne use", but no more. Another interesting clause obliged him to "leve the warren well replenished with 2,000 conyes or more to be determined by the discreton of four persons indifferently to be chosen" by the parties to the agreement at the end of the term. Presumably the warren continued to be exploited in the following two centuries, for in a lease of Westwood Farm, commencing in November 1701 the landlord permitted the tenant, Nathaniel fflowardow, to:

> "have the use of the warren as well upon the walks (i.e. sheepwalks, heathlands) as in the inclosures until St James' day right before the expiration of the lease. And the said Nathaniel fflowardow doth for himself and his heirs executors and assigns hereby covenant and grant that he or they (during the said term) shall deliver weekly from St. James's day to Candlemas three score rabbits to Cookfield Hall."

Thus some 1,500 rabbits per year were sent to the hall in part payment of rent, so the total production of the warren was probably several times this figure.

The lease was renewed in 1706 for a further period under the same terms, but half a century later the warren seems to have been less fully exploited. Indeed, it is not specifically mentioned in a lease beginning in October 1764, the landlord simply reserving the liberty "to take coneys, game, and wildfowl upon the premises" for himself.

"Coney" and "Warren" are quite common place-names in east Suffolk. There is a Coney Hill at Benacre and another at Henham. Warren Hill appears as a field name in Leiston parish. As in Breckland, many areas of heathland carry the designation warren — near Aldeburgh and north of Southwold for example. Snape Warren, a stretch of heath inland from Aldeburgh which presents a dazzling splash of yellow gorse and broom flowers in summer has two low turf ridges running along one margin which may represent what remains of the double trapping-bank of the former coney-warren.

In both Breckland and the Sandlings, as has already been suggested, sheep and rabbits grazed from the same area of heath. A document dated 1576 describes the manor of Benacre, and about 200 acres (80ha) of the lord's warren is mentioned as being "now replenished" with both sheep and coneys. Other sources of eighteenth and nineteenth century date confirm that this dual use was common practice. An interesting ecological relationship existed between the sheep and the rabbits; one witness before the Parliamentary Committee enquiring into the game laws in 1872 said of a Breckland warren:

"The sheep and rabbits . . . feed well together, because there is a certain portion that the sheep will take, and another portion that the rabbits will take . . . the warren will by nature produce a certain something which the sheep will browse upon in wet weather, and a fine short grass that the rabbits will feed upon but where the sheep can scarely live."

The "certain something" was probably the lichen *Cladonia* — another witness described it as "a species of white moss". Many studies have shown that heavy grazing of heathland by rabbits suppresses many of the grasses and other flowering plants so that eventually little remains except sand sedge (*Carex arenaria*), lichens and mosses. The relationship was not a simple one however, as there was a certain amount of competition between the sheep and rabbits and some shepherds were strongly of the opinion that the mosses and lichens were not altogether good for their flocks.

A striking reduction in the numbers of sheep has been one of the most fundamental changes in East Anglian agriculture in recent decades. Within the memory of many folk now living the sight of a shepherd guiding a flock across the expanses of purple heather was a familiar sight. During the lambing season the shepherd has to stay close to his sheep and he sometimes lived in a small wooden hut on wheels, a primitive caravan that was drawn to the heaths by horses. Although few have been used since the 1930s, some of these serving as tool-sheds or hen-houses can still be seen in allotments and gardens in the east Suffolk heathland zone. But between 1938 and 1962, for example, the number of sheep kept in east Suffolk fell by two thirds. The war-time and post-war emphasis on arable production in the eastern counties, the very high costs of labour for folding sheep and the impossibility of obtaining shepherds are quoted as explanations, but the decline had already begun in the 1920s.

The virtual disappearance of the sheep, the central element in a system that had remained stable for several centuries, had far-reaching consequences. No longer were the heaths, lowland pastures and arable lands complementary to one another. Instead a pattern developed of entirely separate land-use elements — arable land, forestry plantation, golf-course, airfield, gravel-workings, pasture, and, in the coastal heathland area, saltmarsh — with few ecological or economic connections between them. The heaths, when their ecological link with the surrounding land-use elements was severed, instead of being an important element in a complex and integrated system temporarily became almost useless.

The total area of heathland in the Suffolk Sandlings has been decreasing for at least two centuries, but in the last three decades the rate has greatly accelerated. Eighteenth century maps show large tracts of heath covering most of the area between Ipswich and Lowestoft. In 1889 there were 19,000 acres (7,700ha) of heathland in the region; by 1966 this had been reduced to about 8,400 acres (3,400ha). 2,984 acres (1,200ha) have been reclaimed in that part of the region between the estuaries of the Alde and the Orwell since 1949. The reduction in the area of heath in Breckland has been equally dramatic.

There are several reasons, some technical, others economic, for the recent expansion of arable agriculture at the expense of the heaths. The benefits of summer irrigation in an area of very light sandy soils and of low rainfall were realised and it was a Sandlings farmer who, in 1947, was the first in Britain to use this technique. Two dry summers in the late 1950s greatly stimulated interest and there are now many farmers who use irrigation to increase their yields of potatoes and sugar beet on light soils. Trace element deficiencies were also to be expected on the highly leached sandy soils of the heathland area. Boron deficiency in sugar beet was corrected and poor growth of cereals and root crops was recognised as being the result of low levels of magnesium and copper in the soil. These problems were overcome in the 1950s. There have also been developments in the techniques used for spreading lime, fertilisers and pesticides.

A farmer reclaiming heath is also in a favourable position in regard to obtaining subsidies. Liming is often required on sandy heathland soils and farmers can obtain a contribution towards the cost of acquiring, transporting and spreading approved liming materials. A subsidy is also available for many types of fertiliser, and a grant may be claimed for ploughing "difficult" land. Until recently funds were available for eliminating bracken from pastoral land. Margins of profit on reclaimed heathland in East Anglia are not high, but are considered satisfactory as in almost every case reclaimed land is farmed in association with existing large holdings; very light soils can often be ploughed or drilled when heavier land on other parts of the farm cannot be worked.

The increase of forestry in the heathland areas of east Suffolk and Breckland and the ecological effect of afforestation has already been described (Chapter Three).

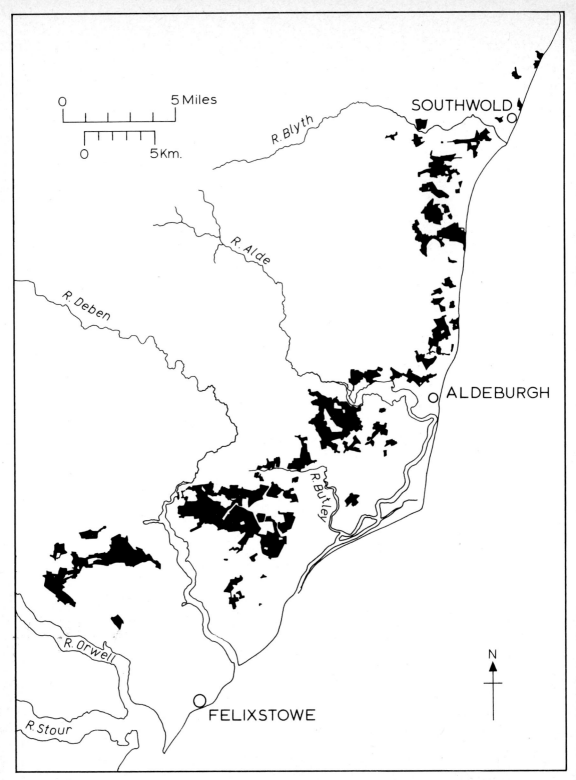

Figures 34 and 35. The reduction in the area of heathland in the Sandlings of Suffolk between

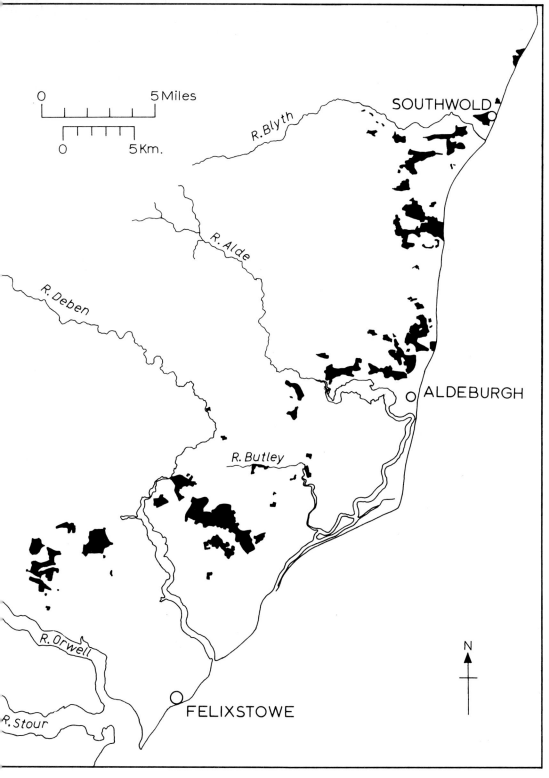

1889 and 1966.

Urban development has significantly reduced the area of heathland in some parts of lowland England; London has engulfed many of the Surrey heaths, the Portsmouth—Southampton conurbation some of those of the Hampshire Basin and Bournemouth—Poole those of Dorset. The East Anglian heaths have experienced this type of invasion to a slightly lesser extent, but Ipswich has expanded in the direction of the heaths of the southern Sandlings, and Thetford in Breckland, along with Mildenhall and Brandon, have become associated with the Greater London Council "expanding towns" ("overspill") scheme. Demand for sand and gravel usually accompanies building development. Mineral workings have an important effect on amenity locally, for example at Westleton in east Suffolk, but the total area of heathland in East Anglia affected in this way is not large. In any event, heathland plants and animals reinvade the workings quite soon after abandonment. Some small pits dug on Walberswick Common in 1952 had a well-established filigree of heather spreading over the bare sand three years later. Two species of heathland reptile (the lizard and adder) were present along with a number of heathland butterflies. It has even been argued that abandoned mineral workings provide a greater range of microhabitat and therefore show a more varied assemblage of species than undisturbed heathland.

The Defence Departments made considerable use of the open heaths of eastern England in both World Wars. In the First War, for example, a bombing target was outlined on Lakenheath Warren for a Royal Flying Corps squadron based at Feltwell. A rough outline of a warship was also scraped on a north-facing slope for guns on Wangford Warren. In the Second World War a dummy airfield was constructed on Eriswell Low Warren, the lights being controlled from dugouts at Lakenheath. Dummy concrete tanks were also set up and part of the heathland was used to store bombs. Tank training took place both on Breckland heaths and on those of east Suffolk. Indeed substantial areas of Breckland are still controlled by the military in the Thetford Stamford Battle Area. But as with the scars caused by gravel-workings, time tends to heal wounds inflicted upon the landscape; it may even be the case that disturbance of the soil brings plant nutrients from deeper layers towards the surface, with beneficial effects on the plant community.

In contrast, the construction of airfields causes long-term changes. even in the 1930s such work was having an effect on the ecology and land-use pattern of the region. In 1932 the Suffolk writer C. B. Ticehurst, in his book the *Birds of Suffolk,* makes several references to the effects of "aeronautics" on wildlife. A little over 800 acres (325ha) of Sandlings heathland were used for Martlesham airfield before the Second War and the wartime and post-war requirements of the Defence Departments have led to the establishment of R.A.F. Woodbridge and R.A.F. Bentwaters. Much of the land taken for the long runways at Woodbridge was Forestry Commission plantation, although it had been heathland a couple of decades previously.

Approaching 1,500 acres of former heathland has been taken for Golf Courses. Important periods of links construction were towards the end of the nineteenth century (Aldeburgh and Southwold, 1884, Purdis Heath, Ipswich, 1895) and in the 1920s (Rushmere Heath Ipswich, 1927). Both these were periods of agricultural recession, when substantial tracts of farmland were reverting to heath and the value of the heaths was very low. The ecological effects of a change in land use from open heathland to golf course are difficult to assess. Patches of grass-heath and gorse may be retained as rough, and among these typical heathland species of insect and reptile may be found. Grazing (apart from that of rabbits) may be eliminated from such areas and they are protected from fire. There is thus a tendency for gorse to grow up and form what is almost a single species plant community, or for patches of heather to be invaded by birch and pine. Almost continuous human disturbance will result in the avoidance of the area by many species of birds for which the habitat might otherwise be suitable. However, at Thetford, where most of the heaths are now covered by conifer plantations, the Golf Course provides almost the only patch of unforested land for some miles.

In spite of the emphasis on recent changes in the foregoing, it must not be thought that the reduction in the areas of heathland is entirely a recent phenomenon; it has continued for several centuries. As early as 1795 Arthur Young wrote of the Sandlings, "All these heaths will disappear in time" for even in his day reclamation was continuing apace. But periods of consolidation or even of retreat have marked stages in the general advance of the arable land into the heaths. Maps exist showing the distribution of heathland as a group of parishes — Chillesford, Butley, Tunstall and Eyke in east Suffolk in 1600 (the Norden Survey of the Estate of Sir Michael Stanhope) and for the same area at the time of the Tithe Surveys in 1840. There had been a marked reduction in the total area of heath in the period, but isolated instances of reversion. Indeed, the Assistant Tithe Commissioner for Benacre recorded that quite substantial acreages of the lighter lands had been withdrawn from the plough, and were falling back to heathland in the 1840s. The Tithe Apportionments for Rushmere St Andrew, near Ipswich, are also interesting; there are several altered apportionments subsequent to that of 1845. The 1845 document shows heathland divided into large enclosures, some of which had been brought into arable cultivation, others remaining as open heath. By 1899 several changes had occurred in the southern part of the parish; some of the arable land had reverted to sheepwalk, but other areas of heath had come under the plough. A detailed study of air photographs and a comparison of First Land Utilisation Survey material (1930s) with more recent data show that the same thing has been happening on a small scale in recent years.

In Breckland, too, the boundary between heathland and arable has long been a fluctuating one. A map of West Wretham, Norfolk, made in 1741, now owned by King's College, Cambridge, illustrates what was probably a typical system of land management for the period. The arable land of a Breckland village was divided into two parts; a small "infield", cropped continuously, close to the settlement, and a larger "outfield" comprising about eight temporary enclosures from the heath. These areas, called "brakes" on the Wretham map, were cultivated intermittently. One would be broken each year, cropped for a few seasons, with the aid of sheep manure and marling (see Chapter Seven), and then be allowed to revert to heathland until its turn came to be ploughed again. W. G. Clarke, in his classic book *In Breckland Wilds* wrote, "parts of almost every area of heathland were at one time cultivated, but have become derelict. Both these areas and the large sandy open fields are known as 'brecks', and their number, and the fact that they are characteristic of all parishes, induced me in 1894 to give the district the name of Breckland". However, the term "The Brock District" seems to have been used for some decades previously.

It is difficult for the visitor of today, passing through mile after mile of the dark green Corsican pine plantations of the modern Breckland to imagine what the area must have been like a century or two ago as a wilderness of bracken and heather, broken by stretches of grass-heath and occasional clumps of yellow-flowering gorse, stretching almost to the horizon in every direction. Almost the only contrast with the gentle curves of the dry valleys and sand dunes was provided by the clumps of Scots pine trees silhouetted against the sky. The great tracts of bare flints that formed where the wind had removed the light topsoil, provided ideal sites for nesting stone curlews (*Burhinus oedicnemus*) and nightjars (*Caprimulgus europaeus*). The adult birds of both species, when squatting on the nest are almost invisible, so closely does their plumage resemble the withered bracken fronds and lichen covered wood fragments that cover the heathland soil. When the sitting bird at length flies up from the nest there is a striking similarity of the blotched eggs to the oval flints nearby. And as late as 1812 there was a drove of 50 great bustard (*Otis tarda*) at Icklingham; this splendid bird — the male is 40in (100cm) in length and is one of the largest land birds in Europe has long moustachial bristles and a bright rufous neck-band — last nested in Breckland in 1832. Overhunting was responsible for its extermination. Outside Britain it is a bird of steppes and treeless plains; because of the destruction and fragmentation of the open heaths it seems unlikely that it will ever breed again in East Anglia, although an attempt was made to reintroduce it at Elveden in 1906.

Figure 36. Heathland bird: the nightjar (*Caprimulgus europaeus*).     E. A. Armstrong

Figure 37. Heathland bird: the stone curlew (*Burhinus oedicnemus*).  E. A. Armstrong.

Another spectacular bird that was not uncommon on Breckland heaths in the early years of the nineteenth century was the kite (*Milvus milvus*). Indeed, at that time the Falconers Society used to fly their falcons at kites at Eriswell, Barton Mills and Brandon. Alas, persecution and habitat destruction have long since eliminated the kite, along with several other heathland species. The Dartford warbler (*Sylvia undata*), a small heathland bird with a purple-brown breast and slate-grey upper parts, was never, as far as in known, found in the Brecks but seems to have been present in small numbers on several of the coastal heaths of east Suffolk up to the turn of the century. It was found on a heath near Woodbridge in 1914, from which it was burnt out the following year, and near Sudbourne in 1916. The severe winter of 1917 seems to have reduced numbers substantially for there are few records for the years that follow. A very small number of watchers claimed to have seen the species in east Suffolk in the 1920s, the last record for East Anglia being from heathland near Walberswick in 1939.

The populations of many species of heathland bird have declined spectacularly in recent years. The stone curlew was breeding in appreciable numbers in almost every coastal parish from the Orwell estuary to Covehithe in 1956, but in recent years only four pairs have bred. Other species—the stonechat, whinchat, woodlark and wheatear have also decreased. The populations of several reptiles and an amphibian—the natterjack toad (*Bufo calamita*) have been reduced, and some heathland insects such as the silver-studded blue butterfly have a much more reduced distribution.

One factor that has been disadvantageous to heathland wildlife has been the great increase in recreational pressure on unenclosed land of all types; a consequence of this has been the intermittent starting of quite serious fires. In recent years in east Suffolk, for example, there has been an average of over 70 heathland fires per year. In the year 1st April 1967 — 31st March 1968 there were 106 fires and 438 acres (190ha) were affected. These burnings are not, of course entirely a recent phenomenon. Ticehurst wrote (in 1932) ". . . few years pass that there is not a disastrous fire on one or more of the commons." The fires are often started by visitors throwing down a lighted cigarette, or abandoning a picnic fire before it is properly extinguished. Such a heath fire started on 15th April 1968 (Bank Holiday Monday) on Dunwich Heath. About 25 acres (10.2ha) heathland were burned before the fire spread onto the nearby Minsmere Bird Reserve. In all about 83 acres (33.6ha) were affected.

It is rather difficult to differentiate between the effects of grazing and burning since they interact; the disappearance of the sheep from many of the heaths in the 1920s and 30s led to the cessation of the *controlled* burning that had accompanied the grazing, and it is possible that the fierce *uncontrolled* blazes caused by accident over the last few decades have had a rather different ecological effect from the fires which were formerly lit on some of the heaths to burn away the older fibrous heather and provide young shoots as food for sheep. There is some evidence that when heather over fifteen years old is burnt, the woody stems generate sufficient heat to damage the roots. Regeneration then has to take place from seed, and bracken, in particular, may invade before the heather can grow up again. A fierce uncontrolled blaze on mature stands of heather may hasten the invasion of a birch-bracken assemblage. Such a fire has a rather different effect from the controlled fires on areas that were regularly grazed and where the heather plants were smaller.

Another complex series of changes in the ecology of the heaths followed the outbreak of myxomatosis (rabbit disease) in East Anglia. The virus was first reported in East Anglia from Easton Bavents in Suffolk on 2nd December, 1953, after appearing in Kent in October of that year. There were outbreaks in many parts of Norfolk and Suffolk in the spring 1954 and by the end of that year there were few parts of the two counties that were not affected although the spread into Cambridgeshire was rather slower.

As grazing by stock on the heaths had ended about twenty-thirty years previously, the elimination of the rabbit resulted in substantially higher growth of grass from about 1955 onwards and the rapid acceleration, on almost every heath, of the invasion of gorse and bracken and very often birch and pine as well. Many areas of heathland both in the Breck and the Sandlings are now dotted with pine trees 12-15 feet high and up to twenty years old. Lichens, formerly important constituents of the heathland flora decreased with the reduction in rabbit pressure.

The reduction in rabbit numbers was dramatic: on one estate 5,025 rabbits are recorded in the game book as being killed in the season 1953-4, but only 35 the following year. Game records also reveal that the stoat almost completely disappeared, although there is evidence that an early effect of the elimination of the rabbit was the deflection of food-chains, and there were reports that in both 1954 and 1955 there was increased predation on ground-nesting birds such as the wheat ear. A number of other heathland bird species, the stonechat (*Saxicola torquata*) for example, depend on open grassy areas for food, and myxomatosis may have contributed towards their decline. The initial effect on some heathland insects, such as the small and Essex skipper butterflies (*Adopoea sylvestris* and *A. lineola*), was beneficial; it seems that with the removal of the rabbit the favourite food-plant of the larvae, the cat's tail grass (*Phleum nodosum*) was allowed to grow without disturbance. In the longer term, however, scrub invaded the open areas and the silver studded blue (*Plebejus argus*), for example, which as recently as 1952 was described as "common on the heaths of east Suffolk" was found only in small numbers in one or two localities by the 1960s. It is important to appreciate that because of the economic and other changes described above, not only has the total areas of heathland been substantially reduced, but it has become progressively more fragmented. As the former large expanses of heathland became broken up, and the small heaths widely spaced, birds, in particular, may be restricted in their breeding by the fact that individuals have difficulty in finding mates. Also, while a single heath may not provide sufficient food for a brood of young, movement between several heaths would be very wasteful of time and energy. It is also possible that where a very low population exists the level of social stimulation may not be sufficient to induce breeding. The changes in status of many heathland organisms can thus most clearly be understood in the context of the complex of inter-related changes in the East Anglian coutryside as a whole.

Special efforts are being made to conserve the fragments of open heathland that remain. In east Suffolk, near Westleton, 117 acres (45ha) of heath have been managed by the Nature Conservancy since 1956, and more recently 1210 acres (486ha) of marsh and heathland between the villages of Walberswick and Blythburgh have been designated as National Nature Reserves. In Breckland, Weeting and Thetford Heaths are National Nature Reserves. The Royal Society for the Protection of Birds has also been active in the conservation of East Anglia's heaths: their Minsmere reserve, adjoining Westleton Heath, contains substantial areas of heath, and the Society also manages Aldeburgh Warren, a few miles to the south. Close to Minsmere is an area of 214 acres (87ha) of heathland and cliff which has been property of the National Trust since 1967. A number of heaths have been designated Sites of Special Scientific Interest (S.S.S.I.), for example Snape Warren. Designation of an area as an S.S.S.I. does not involve any change in the ownership of the land, but places a duty on the local Planning Authority to consult with the Nature Conservancy if any change in the use of the land is envisaged. Much of the coastline north of the River Debden has been included in the Suffolk Coast and Heaths Area of Outstanding Natural Beauty by the Countryside Commission, and special Planning procedures apply to it.

Norfolk was the first county to have a County Naturalists Trust; it was founded in 1925. It is appropriate that a monument to the founder, the late Dr Sydney Long, should stand on one of the most attractive areas of heathland in the county, and a stone commemorating this pioneer of East Anglian conservation stands close to Langmere on the Trust's East Wretham Heath Reserve.

CHAPTER SIX

# Lanes and Trackways

". . . the drovers' lanes . . . make some of the quietest walking in England."

"Is there anything uglier in the whole landscape than an arterial by-pass road, except an airfield?"

W. G. Hoskins
*The Making of the English Landscape*

THE MOTORIST speeding along the gently undulating roads of Norfolk or Suffolk is sometimes required to turn his vehicle sharply as the surface of the carriageway makes an abrupt, right-angled bend. Often at such a corner an unmetalled track or bridleway continues, following the alignment of the modern motor road. Were he to get out of his car, the motorist might discover a trackway, half-hidden beneath a hedge-to-hedge counterpane of white fools' parsley flowers in early summer, running many miles across country. If he carried an Ordnance Survey map in his car our traveller might find that the lane he had just examined eventually petered out. However, were he to lay a ruler along the representation of the track on a 1 inch or 2½ inch sheet, he might discover that the straight-edge was running along another stretch or road, trackway or simply a footpath some distance further on. In such a manner Peddars Way may be traced across the entire county of Norfolk, from Rushford in the Little Ouse valley to the coast near Hunstanton. But sometimes not even a footpath remains, for an unmade-up trackway soon disappears if ploughed over in light soiled areas. Even so the former course of a routeway may be traced, here in the ruler-straight margin of a wood or plantation (as with Peddars Way on Brettenham Heath), there in a field or parkland boundary (as in the eastern edge of the park at Eleveden Hall, Suffolk, which abuts onto the Icknield Way). East Anglia is criss-crossed by the remnants of early lines of communication, once important to the region's economy, but long since superseded and so now largely abandoned and half-forgotten.

The alignment of parish-boundaries along a linear feature is a sure sign of its antiquity. The "Roman Road" of the Gog Magog Hills, extending from Cambridge to Haverhill, is such a case. It is perhaps of pre-Roman origin but was improved in Roman times towards the Cambridge end, and forms a boundary between the parishes along 10 miles of its length. In places where former roads are invisible on the ground, or even from the air, the dotted symbol representing a parish boundary on an Ordnance Survey map may provide evidence of their former existence. Sometimes the previous course of a road that has been straightened, or shifted laterally a few yards to avoid an obstruction such as a fallen tree sometime in the past can be discerned in this way.

The Icknield Way is surely the best known of East Anglia's ancient trackways. It has its beginnings in the Chalk hills of Wessex, where it passes Stonehenge and countless other classic sites of the Salisbury Plain heartland of so much of pre-historic culture in Britain. South of Swindon a loop sweeps as a "green road", the Berkshire Ridgeway, over the chalky heights above the Vale of the White Horse, passing by Uffingdon Castle, an Iron Age Hillfort. North of the Thames, in the Chiltern Hills, the Icknield Way is a two-fold feature; the Upper Icknield Way running still as a grassy ridgeway along the crest of the escarpment, a lower route hugging the foot of the scarp face, for use when the higher road was impassable. The course of the Way is followed by A505 at the base of steep Chalk slopes in Hertfordshire, but becomes a rough trackway again as it makes its way across rather featureless country north-east of Royston. Frequently the point where it crossed a river is emphasised in a place name, such as Thetford or Lackford, but such names are usually much younger than the routeway itself. Some sort of ferry-system may have been in operation over the Wash, then probably narrower than at present, when wayfarers first trod the Icknield Way, for it seems to continue northwards in another routeway in the Lincolnshire Wolds.

Figure 38. The Icknield Way, Norfolk.                    *P. H. Armstrong*

*Tumuli* are seldom far away in Chalk country; there is a scattering of them not far from the Way near Royston, and in its Bedfordshire section, the Icknield Way passes Galley Hill, which has an interesting, if rather gruesome history. Two burial mounds here have been excavated—both were constructed in the Neolithic. Underneath one of them fragments of pottery were found, in which were impressions of wheat grains. Beneath the other were the remains of two young men whose bodies had been dismembered before interment. Much later a group of men, women and children were slaughtered on the hilltop and their remains also buried in the Neolithic mound. This probably happened in A.D. 367, when there was a co-ordinated attack on Britain from Hadrian's Wall to the Thames by the Saxons, the Picts from Scotland and the Scots of Ireland. Subsequently Galley Hill had a gallows on its summit. There are also Neolithic long barrows on West Rudham and Hapley Commons in Norfolk.

The presence of literally hundreds of pre-historic antiquities close to the Icknield Way—it passes within a mile or two of the Neolithic flint mines at Grime's Graves—cannot be coincidential. When was it first used? What is its significance? It is certainly pre-historic, perhaps four or five thousand years old. We have seen how Neolithic and Bronze Age cultivators preferred the light lands to the heavier clay, and so the chalklands of the "Ichnield Way Belt" from the Salisbury Plain to the Wash had a much higher density of population than either the glacial till plateau of high Norfolk and Suffolk to the east or the damp valleys to the west. (See Chapter Two and the reference to Neolithic wheat in Bedfordshire, above.) Probably there was considerable movement and trade along this corridor in the two or three millennia before the arrival of the Romans; certainly, in spite of the importance of the Grime's Graves industry, Neolithic stone axes imported from Cornwall, Wales, Teesdale and Great Langdale in the Lake District have been found quite close to the Way in Norfolk, Suffolk and Cambridgeshire.

The importance of the Icknield Way corridor in Anglo-Saxon times, when numerous dykes were thrown up to block it has also already been shown.

When the Romans came to Britain they required an efficient, planned network of routes, passable in all weathers, for the transport of troops, stores and officials. The roads were laid out by military engineers, usually in straight stretches, by sighting between prominent points, although the routes are often not straight over long distances. Sometimes, as in the case of a portion of the Icknield Way, the courses of earlier trackways were followed. The most important roads were built of layers of stones mixed with earth; usually large stones were laid in an excavated bed, with finer gravel or flint above and kerbs holding the metalling in place. It is these stones, where they lie scattered over the surface of the soil, that can betray the Roman roads that have been disused for many centuries. For example, Peddars Way, after crossing from Norfolk into Suffolk, is traceable in Coney Weston parish as a long light scar across the arable fields. Further south, where this old Roman

Road forms the boundary between the parishes of Barningham and Bardwell, a prominent hedgerow marks the route once taken by squads of marching soldiers.

The metalled portion of the road might be 15-20 feet wide, but there was sometimes a grass verge on either side for horsemen. A long undisturbed strip of grassland fringes the white stony trackway of the Roman Road on the Gog Magog Hills and here, where the hooves of the Centurions' horses once trod, many native chalkland plants and insects survive. The writer vividly remembers his pleasure on finding the sky blue flowers of perennial flax (*Linum anglicum*) amidst the short grasses close to the Cambridge end of this road. The possible ecological role of the Roman road system as a vehicle for the dispersal of imported weeds has been mentioned in Chapter Two.

Figure 39. The course of Peddars Way can be traced in the crop-marks and hedges near Coney Weston, Suffolk. Note also the rectangular landscape of eighteenth century enclosures and the regularly spaced marl-pits. *Cambridge University Collection*

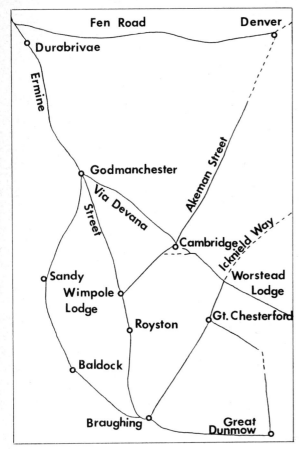

Figure 40. Sketch-map showing the Roman roads of the Cambridge region. *After J. Liversidge, British Association for the Advancement of Science, Cambridge Survey 1965.*

The Roman network of roads around Cambridge is quite well known, but note that the name *Via Devana* (now the A604) was coined by an academic in the nineteenth century. Elsewhere the pattern is less clear. Doubtless in the future a peculiar regularity of parish boundaries, a straight stretch of hedgerow or the slight discoloration of a ploughed field will reveal the presence of roads whose existence is at present conjectural. But Norman Scarfe has suggested that on well-drained soils a thick foundation was unnecessary. He argues that the reason why there appear to be so few roads across the Suffolk coastal heaths towards the Roman settlements at Dunwich and Aldeburgh was that the usual method for the construction of highly durable roads was not employed. The sandy tracks that run straight through the bracken and heather may be all that remain of Roman roads.

This problem of the absorption of Roman roads back into the landscape seems also to have beset students of an intriguing network of local roads along the north Norfolk coast. From Holme-next-the-Sea to Brancaster a rectangular pattern of roads divided the land into remarkably evenly-shaped parcels. Many of the occupation roads between them have dissolved into the sandy soil, but some remain as hedgebanks. A map made in 1609 shows rather more of the rectilinear pattern than can be seen today. The system is bounded on the east by the Roman Peddars Way, by the Parish boundary running along the Green Bank trackway to the south and peters out into saltmarsh, much of which has accreted since Roman times, to the north. Several finds of Romano British pottery in the area would appear to confirm the association.

Roman roads often run for many miles without passing through villages — Peddars Way, for instance, does not pass through any settlements of appreciable size between Castle Acre and Ringstead, a distance of 17 miles (27km). Saxon villages were set off the roads partly for security from raiders, partly it is said, because the colonisers feared that the mysterious, long, straight trackways were haunted! In any event Fring, Docking and Great and Little Massingham (all " —ing" villages) are a mile or so off the route of Peddars Way. There were exceptions, however; one of them is Arrington, "the farm of the people of Earna", or Ermine Street (now the A10 at this point) in Cambridgeshire. This road, once the main Roman route from London to the northern military capital at York, also takes its name from *Earningas* — Earna's folk.

The Roman roads were neglected and deteriorated in the centuries that followed the cutting of the link with Rome. Some of them went out of use entirely, replaced in the Middle Ages by other routes between East Anglia's growing towns. Most roads were rutted and travel was difficult. In winter it must have been often little less than nightmarish. In 1555 parishes were given the duty of maintaining the roads within their boundaries, both highways and by-ways, but the scheme was not a success. The experience of a French landowner, the Duc de la Rochefoucauld, who visited east Suffolk in 1784, is entirely typical. He wrote of a journey by coach across the heathland north of the River Deben: "The further we went the deeper we found ourselves in soft sands, which was tiring for our horses and made it difficult . . . to move." The system of local support continued until the Local Government Act of 1888, and in many an East Anglian parish, where the fields were stony but where road-building material was scarce, this was associated with the back-breaking task of the "stone-picking" of the fields by the poor. The removal of stone was said to improve crop yields, but an experiment once conducted on the flint-strewn fields of the Suffolk Sandlings in which the same quantity of seed was applied to both cleared and uncleared land resulted in the field that had not been "stone-picked" producing the better crop!

In the eighteenth century turnpike trusts were established to repair stretches of old highway and occasionally to construct new ones, using the improved methods of road-constructions of Thomas Telford and John Macadam. The road was paid for by the charging of tolls; at each end of a stretch of highway it was barred by a "turnpike", a revolving pole set with pikes or spikes, where the tolls were paid to the keeper in his toll-house beside the road. These toll-houses, often miles from any village and with their characteristic hexagonal or octagonal plan, like that on the A134 at Sicklesmere in Suffolk, have been described as the most important compulsory for the turnpike trusts to provide milestones on their roads, and many of trusts merely took over existing roads. An Act of Parliament of 1773 made it compulsory for turnpike trusts to provide milestones on their roads, and many of the stones that survive by East Anglia's roadsides date from the late eighteenth century. However, what are claimed to be the first true milestones in England are two massive structures, one just north of Trumpington on the A10, another a mile closer to Cambridge, giving the distance, two miles and one mile respectively, from Great St Mary's Church. They were put up in 1727.

Although to many travellers the turnpikes were a boon, they were less helpful to drovers with large numbers of animals to move. The stone surfaces wearied the cattle and there might be infuriating delays while the toll-keeper counted the animals passing through the gate, quite apart from the cost. For these reasons a network of drovers' roads grew up, green lanes usually avoiding villages, where stock could graze as they made their unhurried way, southwards perhaps, from Scotland and the hills of northern England to slaughterhouses in centres such as Norwich and London. At intervals along the way were "stances", where the stock were enclosed overnight, often behind an inn where the drovers could obtain refreshment. Traces of these may sometimes be found, even though the inn has long since closed its doors, in a local field- or place-name, e.g. "Wart-an-Dot Piece", Cumbrian or Border dialect for "enclosed pasture with drinking place". Sometimes the drovers used pre-existing trackways, the antiquity of which can be vouched for by the fact that parish boundaries frequently follow them. They usually run parallel to a highway or former turnpike for many miles.

In Huntingdonshire, from a point north of Alconbury on Ermine Street an old cattle drovers' lane, appropriately known as Bullock Road, can be traced northwards for 15 miles via Moonshine Gap and past quaintly named farms such as Cold Harbour, Flittermere Lodge, Ongutein Manor and Tookey Lodge to Elton Furze. Here at a T-junction with the A605, its route becomes difficult to trace. For most of its length Bullock Road is a constant two miles west of the Great North Road. In many places it is a metalled by-road, a narrow strip of macadam between hedges some 20 yards apart, but from time to time the improved surface makes a dog's leg turn leaving the drovers' road as a rutted green lane with the occasional yellow-hammer singing out its rattling "Little-bit-of-bread-and-no-cheese" song above a hedgebank overgrown with teasels (*Dipsacus fullonum*) and thistles. For example, where the modern road turns towards the village of Great Gidding, the old cattle-men's trackway continues as a swathe of green, broken only by the occasional abandoned harrow or plough, half-hidden beneath the climbing bindweed. In places the margin of a wood forms one of the edges of the lane, as in the case of Aversley

Wood and at Glatton Folly and along one stretch it forms the boundary between Huntingdonshire and Northamptonshire. Parishes meet along much of its length and the hedges that border it frequently have a varied shrub flora — all signs of its antiquity.

Maybe cattle did once *ford* the River Nene at Wansford, a few miles north-west of where Bullock Road peters out at Elton Furze, but part of the attractive stone bridge that carries the main street across the river dates from 1577. As this narrow, 12-arched structure was until quite recently the only crossing for several miles in either direction, it must surely have been over it that the drovers chivvied their jostling herds southwards.

A little to the north another drovers' road can be picked up; Sewstern Lane or the Drift runs from Ermine Street near Greeton, north to the River Witham which was probably crossed at a ford north of Foston, and on towards the Trent valley near Newark. This road avoids villages and traffic for long distances and the counties of Leicestershire and Lincolnshire meet along it for nearly 10 miles. It may have existed since the Bronze Age, perhaps being used as a "salt way" in the Middle Ages for the transport of this important commodity by packhorse from the pans of the Lincolnshire coast and inland salt wells (one of these is marked on some old maps at Allington, close to the lane). Sewstern Lane seems to have been used by drovers from about the sixteenth century until the trade declined in the nineteenth.

Watering places were obviously an important consideration when sheep and cattle were being driven long distances. It is therefore no coincidence that another cattle road used extensively in the nineteenth century but also probably pre-historic in origin, passes between Langmere and Ringmere in the Norfolk Breck and then between the expanse of Fowlmere and the enigmatic Devil's Punch Bowl. It makes its way from Peddars Way, or perhaps from East Harling in the east for 15 miles (25km) through what is now conifer plantation but was once dry open heathland to the edge of the Fens at Hockwold cum Wilton.

The effects of the enclosure movement (about 1750-1850) on the landscape have already been described; suffice it to say here that the commissioners, in their enthusiasm for orderliness, often straightened or diverted roads and lanes that had developed almost casually over many centuries as the result of the movement of men and animals from place to place.

Finally there are the roads constructed in the last three or four decades — the arteries of a Britain with 15 million cars. The advent of the container-lorry and the tremendous levels of traffic now experienced on some East Anglian roads in the summer holiday period have resulted in the peace of many a village clinging to former turnpike being cruelly shattered. Few who have tried to manipulate a vehicle through the mediaeval street pattern of Bury St Edmunds on an August Saturday can question the wisdom of constructing a by-pass. Kings Lynn has already been relieved in this way and Norwich's provincial elegance is probably considerably enhanced by the A1074 ring-road which, although it sweeps indiscriminately through patches of open country and suburban fringe alike, protects the ancient city's heart by filtering through traffic away from it.

Roads, therefore, are ubiquitous. They cross a complete range of countryside types and have their origin in every period from the Neolithic to the 1970s. Frequently when the boundaries of a highway were delimited by a hedge or fence a narrow strip of a heathland or meadow community was included as a roadside verge. In the centuries since some of the oldest of East Anglia's verges came into being commons have been reclaimed and former pasture has been ploughed as land everywhere in lowland Britain came under increasing pressure. The strips of land by the side of roads may thus be relict communities, surviving fragments of habitats that have entirely disappeared from the area surrounding them. Certain verges adjacent to the main highways are exposed to heavy pressures: contamination by lead compounds and fumes from cars and lorries, parking of vehicles, dumping of road-metal and grit, illegal encroachment from adjoining farmland, splashing with salty water in the winter and so on. Nevertheless animals and plants of a wide range of habitats — damp pasture, chalk grassland, heath, woodland edge, decaying tree-stumps, pond and ditch — find something of a refuge along many a roadside margin. For several hundred yards along the verges in each direction from the cross-roads at Cherry Hill, south of Barton Mills, Suffolk, a unique assemblage of species typical of Breck grassland can be found. Along the A1065, at Mile End, Brandon, a Breckland speciality, field southernwood (*Artemisia campestris*) still grows although the roadside is much disturbed by the parking of cars and lorries. Across at Witnesham in east Suffolk there is a stretch of verge that retains the characteristics of the woodland-meadow flora once found in nearby fields. But it is not just ancient roadsides that are of ecological interest. Recent road-widening and the construction of a cutting for a dual carriageway on the A11 south of Barton Mills have exposed the underlying chalk, and rapid colonisation by calcicole (lime-loving) plant species has occurred.

Roadside verges require regular cutting to maintain visibility along the highway and to prevent encroachment by scrub, but in Suffolk, at least, an enlightened programme of co-operation between the Nature Conservancy, the County Conservation Trust and the County Surveyors' departments has resulted in the formulation of special management procedures for some 40 stretches of verge that are important ecologically. In many cases, for example, agreement has been reached that lengths of roadside that support interesting plants shall not be cut between May and September.

It might be argued that the road improvers of the eighteenth century served not so much the expanding industry of the nineteenth century, as the motor-orientated society of the twentieth. The first railway trains ran in 1827 and in the

1830s and '40s the East Anglian countryside as well as northern industrial concerns had to make an adjustment to this new mode of transport. A tale is told how a new corn-exchange was built in the Norfolk market town of Swaffham, but was never used as such, as with the arrival of the railway the trade evaporated. But the railways of East Anglia have their own extensive (and emotive) literature and are outside the scope of this book. However railway verges, like roadsides, represent habitats of some consequence and the railways have had appreciable ecological effects; like the network of Roman roads which in some ways it resembles, the railway system has probably facilitated the spread of certain plant species. The Oxford ragwort (*Senecio squalidus*), a plant with bright yellow flower heads was introduced from the stony hills of Sicily and southern Italy to the Oxford Botanic Garden in 1794, but greatly increased its range as the well-drained railway bank habitat became more widespread. Small toadflax (*Chaenorhinum minus*) is another species common as a railway plant in East Anglia, the small seed of this species being spread by the gusts of passing trains. Young plum and apple trees have also been noticed, originating from the stones and cores thrown from carriage windows.

But now the railway system is contracting—much of the formerly extensive network in Norfolk has been axed. Stretches of permanent way have been made into motor-roads or footpaths or returned to cultivation. At Lord's Bridge near Cambridge about 3 miles (5km) of track now carry the eight 42 feet diameter "dishes" of the world's largest radio telescope! Some lengths of track have been made over into nature reserves. In some instances the abandonment of a line has allowed detailed ecological survey of the railway bank environment to be carried out in a way that would have been impossible when diesel locomotives and railcars posed a hazard to the enquirer (or trespasser) examining the side of the track. The long-neglected and sometimes tumbledown walls of some of Eastern Region's station outbuildings and goods' yards have provided sites for ferns only rivalled in the diversity of species found in ancient churchyards! Following the abandonment of the Oxbridge line in 1968, the rare brittle Bladder-fern (*Cystopteris fragilis*) was found growing in a dark, moist "cave" beneath the platform of Old North Road Station platform in Cambridgeshire, along with other species such as Hart's-tongue (*Phyllitis scolopendrium*) and Wall-Rue Spleenwort (*Asplenium ruta-muraria*).

# CHAPTER SEVEN

# Pits and Depressions

"Here pits of crag, with spongy, plashy base,
to some enrich the uncultivated place".

George Crabbe
*The Borough*

THE SUBDUED nature of the countryside of most of East Anglia accentuates any eminence or declivity. A rise in the ground a few metres above the surrounding area or a gentle depression tend to attract attention in the landscape of the eastern counties, whereas elsewhere they would hardly be noticed. Nevertheless it does seem that Norfolk and Suffolk have rather more depressions and pits to the acre than most other parts of Britain. Hugh Prince, in a study of these features in Norfolk found over 27,000 steep-sided depressions on current Ordnance Survey maps, and showed that over a great part of central Norfolk, from Docking and Fakenham, south-eastwards towards Loddon and Diss, there is a zone with 20 pits per square mile (over 8 pits per square kilometer). Air photographs and field studies have shown that in a few areas the density may reach over ten times this figure. Some form conspicuous landscape features—circular or oval clumps of trees in many Norfolk fields conceal depressions—but many have been "ploughed out" and reveal themselves only in a discoloration in the soil or a patch where the sugar-beet has failed.

As so much of East Anglia is underlain by Chalk, the suggestion that some at least of the depressions are the result of the solution of the underlying rock by acidulated rainwater (water in which carbon dioxide and perhaps organic acids from the vegetation and soil is present) is an attractive one. Certainly solution does occur; vertical "pipes" or funnel-shaped masses of sand or clay are sometimes exposed in the sides of chalk quarries—superficial material having fallen into the solution hollows. Splendid examples of these structures were formerly visible in a large quarry near Barton Mills, but continued working of the face has removed them.

There are those who maintain that the Breckland meres (see Chapter Eight) are in solution hollows, possibly enlarged in some cases by the collapse of the surface into underground cavities. But hollows occur so widely in eastern England and in such a variety of materials—sometimes, for example, where a thick layer of glacial till covers the Chalk—that solution of the substratum cannot be the only explanation.

Figure 41. Hollows, probably ground-ice depressions, at Walton Common, Norfolk.

*Cambridge University Collection*

In a belt that extends north-south across west Norfolk and into Cambridgeshire —from Walton Common in the north across Breckland—where Chalk is close to the surface, shallow depressions are particularly common. They range from 30 to over 300 ft in diameter and are typically about 10 ft in depth. Many examples, such as those on Walton Common, are surrounded by a slight rampart. The most likely suggestion is that these are "ground-ice" features that formed under periglacial conditions. During the slow freezing of the ground ice tends to segregate into layers, particularly in fine grained sediments in waterlogged localities—the process can be seen in Alaska and parts of the Soviet Arctic today. As the buried masses of ice increase in size the ground is thrust up. Some of the surface material sludges away from the centre of the mound so formed, so that when the ground-ice eventually melts, a depression, surrounded by a low ridge develops. Thin layers of peat inside some of the depressions at Walton have provided fragments of dwarf birch (*Betula nana*) and a pollen assemblage typical of very cold tundra environments. One may surmise that these declivities formed in the last glacial phase (Devensian) or the immediate post-glacial.

Probably quite a number of the pits are man-made. Although East Anglia can hardly be thought of as a rich mineral-bearing region, a wide variety of materials have, in the past, been extracted. Flints have been worked near Brandon since the Neolithic and the intricate pattern of mounds and hollows that resulted gave rise to confusion for many centuries: the Rev. Francis Blomefield, a local antiquary, wrote in his *History of Norfolk,* first published in 1739:

"About the centre of this hundred, two miles east of Weeting . . . is a very curious Danish incampment, in a semi-circular form, consisting of about twelve acres, on the side of a hill or rising ground of marl or chalk. In this space are great numbers of large deep pits, joined in a regular manner, one near to another, in form of a *quincunx,* the largest seeming to be in the centre, where probably the general's or commander's tent was. These pits are dug so deep, and are so numerous, that they are capable not only of receiving a very great army but also of covering and concealing them . . . at the east end of this entrenchment (called in the neighbourhood, the Holes) is a large tumulus . . . which might also have served as a watch-tower . . ."

It was not until 1870, when another, more systematic, clerical enquirer, Canon W. Greenwell, undertook three seasons of excavations on the site, that its true nature was revealed.

Many pits occur in fields some distance from roads, and it seems reasonable to infer some connection with agriculture. "Marling", in fact has long been a factor in the evolution of the landscape of lowland Britain, for Chaucer wrote in *The Miller's Tale* of a student

"Of astromy and he was so impudent
As to stare upwards while he crossed a field,

Figure 42. Till-filled solution depression in chalk.                    *P. H. Armstrong*

Busy foreseeing what the stars revealed;
And what should happen but he fell down flat
Into a marl-pit. He didn't foresee that!"

(Nevill Coghill's translation, 1951.)

Agricultural marling may be defined as the addition of any mineral material dug from beneath the surface to the topsoil with the object of improving the soil's texture or correcting its acidity. Thus "marl" in this sense includes clay, sand and chalk as well as calcareous clay referred to by geologists as marl.

There is evidence of marling in Norfolk and Suffolk in the thirteenth century, and by the end of the seventeenth century it seems to have been quite widely practised by the more progressive farmers seeking to improve the quality of their land. John Kirby, in the first edition of *The Sufolk Traveller* in 1735 estimated that half the total area of the Sandlings of east Suffolk consisted of heathland, but that large areas were being "converted to good arable land by that excellent manure (crag)". There is confirmation in the court rolls of local manors. The rolls of the manor of Butley, for example, (now in the British Museum) tell of one John May, who, in October 1735 was brought before the Court Baron, it being alleged that he "hath not railed in those pits wherein he hath dugg for Cragg."

Arthur Young, the eighteenth century agricultural writer, had much to say on the subject of cragging and marling in the same area:

"In a part of the maritime sand district called the Sandlings which are south of Woodbridge, Orford and Saxmundham they formerly made great improvement by spreading shell-marl on the black, ling heaths with which all that tract was covered . . . The marl, called there crag, is all dry powdered shells."

Fifty years later another observer was able to summarise the situation in these terms:

"The admixture of the subsoil with the surface has more than anything else contributed to place cultivation of the light lands of Norfolk and Suffolk in the first rank in the scale of farming."

H. Raynbird, in his essay published in 1849, went on to say that some 40-50 cubic yards of marl or clay per acre might be distributed over the fields and that prizes were given, in the years following 1834, by an Agricultural Society for the tenant farmer who marled the greatest portion of his land; one farmer spread 51,789 loads of marl, each of 24 bushels, on an area of 183 acres (74 ha) of arable! It cost him £463.6.9½d. The cost of carting was naturally the largest expense in such an enterprise, and marl pits were sometimes situated at the highest point in a field, to ease spreading.

It is not very often that one can pin-point today the actual marl pits referred to in documents. Lodge Farm, Castleacre, one of the properties owned by the well known Norfolk exponent of improved husbandry methods in the eighteenth century, Thomas Coke, is an example of a holding where this correlation can be made. Holkham estate documents record that in the five years from 1750 to 1754 over 5,000 loads of marl were spread at a cost of over £65, nevertheless in the years that followed much of the land remained in rather poor condition. In 1822 a James Hudson junior obtained a 21-year lease at a low rental; he marled the whole of the farm, manuring it regularly after each crop. He renewed the lease in 1838 and again marled the land. Although much of the property was regarded locally as "very poor, inferior land", in 1851 the farm was reported on as follows: "That such lands produce this enormous bulk of roots and corn is truly astonishing and proves most indisputably the high condition of the farm". Maps made of Lodge Farm in 1816 and 1844 clearly show marl pits; some of these may still be identified as such but many are just shallow depressions. We may be fairly certain that quite a large proportion of the declivities that form a hazard for the inexperienced tractor-driver in East Anglia are partially infilled marl pits.

Coprolites were also worked as a source of fertiliser, particularly in the second third of the nineteenth century. They contain about 53 per cent calcium phosphate and were sometimes burnt before being applied to the land. *White's Directory of Suffolk* records under the entry for Bawdsey:

"Immense quantities of COPROLITE are got in all parishes on or near the coast from Bawdsey Haven to Boyton. It is a valuable mineral, and is extensively used as manure . . . by Suffolk farmers. Its name *coprolite* or *dung-stone* is expressive of its fertilising qualities."

Coprolites were also dug in Cambridgeshire from the Cambridge Greensand, a thin layer between the Gault Clay and the Chalk; slight irregularities and a lightish staining of the soil at the foot of a Chalk hillslope almost invariably indicate former coprolite workings in Cambridgeshire. The ground near Barton, for example, and north of Madingley, has an almost mottled appearance, so numerous were the workings. The depressions themselves are often barely perceptible but on walking across a recently ploughed field one can often pick up several dozen of the dark, slightly shiny coprolites, elongate in form and 2-4 inches (approx. 5-10cm) in length, that were so eagerly sought in the 1850s and '60s.

Figure 43. Dressing coprolites for use as fertiliser, Waldringfield, Suffolk 1887.

*Suffolk Photo Survey (Abbot's Hall Museum)*

Building materials have always posed a problem in East Anglia. In south-east Cambridgeshire and in Norfolk and Suffolk flint is quite widely met with in walls and as a facing for buildings — especially the parish churches. In an area where almost any resistant material has to be utilised, rubble — the larger boulders from glacial till mixed with mud — has been used in about thirty churches in Cambridgeshire. In ten churches in the same county "clunch" or Burwell Rock (known as Totternhoe stone in other parts of England) has been used. Clunch, a hard layer in the Lower Chalk is easily weathered but is used quite extensively in the absence of better material. It may be seen in the walls of barns and cottages along the Lower Chalk outcrop — Reach, Swaffham Bulbeck, Swaffham Prior, Burwell, for example — and it was also used for the tracery in the Lady Chapel of Ely Cathedral. In addition clunch was burnt for lime, as at Commercial End, Swaffham Bulbeck, where a lime kiln was offered for sale as part of a larger trading concern in 1824. The large pits on Church Hill, Reach, are typical of clunch pits in the area.

Today building materials are sought on quite a different scale. The London Brick Company has enormous workings — quarries with step-like sides on which draglines take out the Oxford Clay at several levels at once — on the outskirts of Peterborough. A total of about 2 square miles (5 square kilometers) has been affected by the digging of clay for brick-making at Fletton, Woodston and Yaxley south of the city. An aerial ropeway carries clay across the A15 from the pits to the kilns. The Chalk Marl, a layer in the Lower Chalk, contains a substantial quantity of clay which makes it particularly suitable for cement-making and it is worked at large quarries owned by the Portland Cement Group at Cherry Hinton and Barrington near Cambridge. Sand and gravel are worked on a substantial scale along some of the river valleys of the region, for instance those of the Kennett and the Waveney. In the east Suffolk sandy area, by 1968, a total of 317.7 acres (128.4 ha) had planning permission for sand and gravel working; of this 169.9 acres (68.5 ha), much of it in the parishes of Kesgrave, Foxhill and Westleton, was being worked or was worked out.

While pits and quarries are being actively exploited they provide homes for few animals or plants. What happens when they are abandoned depends partly on the substratum and partly on the height of the water table. Many pits are in fact abandoned just because the cost of pumping eventually becomes prohibitive, so that when the tipper trucks move away and the extraction of water ceases the hollows fill with water. Seeds and fragments of aquatic plants are blown in by the wind, brought on the feet of birds or perhaps artificially introduced. The eggs of water snails and aquatic insects may also arrive along similar routes from nearby pools and ditches. Within a decade an abandoned gravel pit may support both white and yellow water lilies (*Nymphaea alba* and *Nuphar lutea*), and there may be patches of reedswamp invading the shallows — seeds of the reed (*Phragmites communis*) are widely distributed by the wind. A few years later a filigree of willows may surround the pool. Eventually the pit may be partially infilled by the outward growth of vegetation from the margins and the accumulation of silt and dead organic matter on the bottom. Great crested grebes (*Podiceps cristatus*), coot and moorhen are usually breeding in a disused gravel pit within a few years of its abandonment, for example in pits at Milton and Manea in Cambridgeshire and Weybread in Suffolk.

When a Chalk or clunch pit is abandoned a characteristic Chalk grassland community soon develops. In a study of Stapleford parish pit in Cambridgeshire 120 chalkland species of plants were found, including many attractive and sweet-smelling types: blue flax, thyme, and two species of Broomrape (*Orobanche minor* and *O. elatior*)—interesting parasitic species devoid of green colouring that grow on

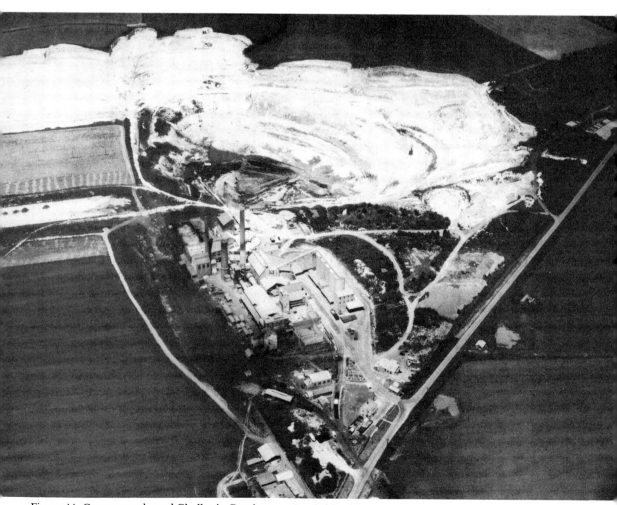

Figure 44. Cement-works and Chalk-pit, Barrington, Cambridgeshire.

*Cambridge University Collection*

the roots of other plants. The large Roman snail (*Helix pomatia*) naturally requires a lot of lime for its shell which may be 40mm high, and is largely confined to chalky areas. It has been claimed that it is found close to the sites of Roman villas and roads, and that this suggests that it was introduced by the Romans, but the correlation may be accidental. Old Chalk pits provide a most suitable habitat for the species. The pit at Harston in Cambridgeshire has been known to be a locality for the Roman snail for over a century; it was the only site in the county where it is found and is apparently the most northerly locality in England. However, in 1972 the local Naturalists Trust collected specimens from the Hertfordshire roadsides where it is abundant and introduced Roman snails to other pits in the area — those at Ickleton, Stapleford and Heydon. At the time of writing (summer 1973) it seems that the new colonies are becoming satisfactorily established.

The sides of many sand pits and old Chalk quarries provide breeding sites for birds such as jackdaws and stock doves, and rather appropriately a colony of sand martins has bred in a disused pit in the grounds of Sandy Lodge, in Bedfordshire, the Headquarters of the Royal Society for the Protection of Birds.

The rapid re-establishment of a heathland community in a worked-out sand and gravel pit was described in Chapter Five.

Quite often the intrinsic interest of the processes of succession or ecological change that follow the abandonment of a quarry or pit is formally recognised by the designation of the site as a nature reserve, usually managed by a Naturalists' or Conservation Trust. In many places in Fenland the drainers dug shallow pits from which clay and/or gravel was obtained for embanking the rivers and drainage channels of the Fens. Such is Bassenhally Pit on the outskirts of Whittlesey. The freehold of the pit is held by the Welland and Nene River Authority, but agreement has been reached whereby a part of the pit is used by a Wildfowlers' Association for clay pigeon shooting and it is also managed as a reserve by the County Naturalists' Trust. A range of habitats is present — freshwater, damp meadow, scrub and copse but of greatest interest is the central depression where water forget-me-not (*Myosotis palustris*), water violet (*Hottonia palustris*) and marsh orchid (*Dactylorchis incarnata*) grow. At least 15 species of birds breed. The pit represents an example of co-operation between bodies and an integrated approach to land use.

Less harmonious were the discussions concerning an old Chalk pit at Little Eversden, Cambridgeshire. Fifteen years of abandonment, up to 1972, had resulted in the growth of an interesting scrub community, and a local outcry followed the ploughing up of the area for winter wheat. The fact of the matter is that in the densely populated south and east of Britain there is severe competition for land of any sort — even old mineral workings. Reclamation for agriculture is often quite possible (as with gravel pits near Conduit Head, Cambridge), and forestry, golf- and shooting-ranges are other uses that have been suggested. Some pits are used for motor-cycle scrambling and "wet" pits are of course widely used by angling clubs and for water-sports.

# CHAPTER EIGHT

# Wetland, Broad and Mere

ONE IS SELDOM far from freshwater in East Anglia. Folk say playfully that Fenmen are born with webbed feet; certainly, as one local historian put it recently, the chug-chug of a diesel engine from an ugly brick and corrugated iron shed in the corner of a remote fen "indicates that the work of drainage initiated by the Romans is still going on". Norfolk has its broads and meres, and the slow rivers of Suffolk that provided inspiration for Constable's paintings still afford a quiet delight to those who amble or fish along their banks.

The reticulate pattern of Fenland drainage channels extends into the chalky south of Cambridgeshire, in the form of ruler-straight "lodes", to the former inland ports at settlements such as Reach, the Swaffhams and Lode. At Reach, now a rather bleak village at the north-west end of the Devil's Ditch, the name The Hythe is still used for an artificial promontory constructed into Reach Lode with basins or private wharves on either side, now partly silted up. Documents tell of Scandinavian timber, coal from north-east England and wine that was brought in here until the nineteenth century. Swaffham Bulbeck Lode runs parallel to Reach Lode a mile and a half (approx. 3km) to the south-west, but in contrast to the situation at Reach, the centre of Swaffham Bulbeck itself is a few hundred yards away from the Fen edge. A separate settlement, appropriately known as Commercial End, now a picturesque curving street of Dutch-style houses and cottages, grew up close to the landing stage. As at Reach, the little basin where the barges formerly unloaded their cargoes of wines and spirits for the Cambridge colleges, bricks, timber, salt and coal is now overgrown and the lode is overhung by willow and elm trees. But the still prosperous-looking Merchant's House, an eighteenth century office or "counting house", the old Granary and the Salt House tell of a business which was described in sale particulars in 1877 as "one of the most capital enterprises in the kingdom".

The railway killed the Fenland barge traffic that had just survived into the first few years of the present century. Dr Ennion, writing of the Fens as they were in the period 1900-1910, describes the scene: "There was always something going on: a string of barges moving massively along the lode, men loading turf, boys fishing." He goes on to mention a whole series of fen industries—turf (peat) cutting, osier gathering, the cutting of sedge and reed for thatchers and eel-fishing with four- or five-pronged eel-glaves or forks. Some of the long, slender withies from the osier bushes (*Salix viminalis*) were woven into tunnel-like eel-traps. The long stems of the true bullrush (*Scirpus lacustris*)—not the reedmace (*Typha latifolia*)—were collected for sale to the coopers; these stalks were placed dry between the barrel staves to keep the joins water-tight. The rural economy of the Fens in those days was closely connected with the wetlands' ecology.

The Fenland environment may now be described in a little more detail. Cambridgeshire north of March, together with adjacent parts of west Norfolk and much of south Lincolnshire is underlain by silts, mineral soils of marine origin. South of this silt fen is the peat fen, where the soils are dark and extremely fertile — five-sixths of all celery grown in England comes from within 20 miles of Ely cathedral. The peats of the "Black Fens" resulted from the incomplete decomposition of plant material under the waterlogged conditions of marshy places in the past. But the situation is more complicated than this simple two-fold division would suggest. Great tracts of land in the area surrounding the Wash lie so close to the sea that the rivers have very little fall and drainage is easily impeded. A trifling rise in sea level can bring salt water far inland and thus there is a complex interdigitation of peats and marine sediments.

About 6-7,000 years ago when the North Sea was dry land, peat began to accumulate in the valleys of some of the Fenland rivers, its formation becoming more general as the climate became damper. Forest — a woodland of pine, oak, elm and hazel — covered the area between the valleys and indeed along the margins of the Fens, as at Woodwalton in Huntingdonshire, a characteristic "brushwood" peat containing much woody, fibrous material was deposited. Above this Lower Peat is the Fen Clay or Buttery Clay, dated by radiocarbon to about 3,000-2,300 B.C. It was deposited in the Neolithic when a rise in the level of the sea brought it far into the Fenland Basin. During the Bronze Age that followed the sea receded and the Upper Peat began to accumulate. This is the peat that is exposed in the southern Fens, but in late Romano-British times there was another brief marine invasion and the surface silts of the northern part of the Fens were laid down.

But in the century or so before this most recent submergence the Romans drained parts of the Fen edges and grew good crops of wheat, much of it destined for the garrison towns of northern England. The Car Dyke was constructed across part of the southern Fens and the remains of Roman settlements can be picked out in air photographs of Cottenham and Chittering. But there was a retreat from Fenland when rising water levels began to make conditions more difficult in about 200 A.D.

In the early mediaeval period Fenland pastures provided grazing for the sheep and cattle owned by several monastic houses and indeed small areas seem to have been used for arable. Small scale drainage ventures were the rule in the fourteenth and fifteenth centuries, with little in the way of an overall plan or the integration of the different schemes. In the sixteenth century came the Dissolution of the religious houses; the period of monastic ownership of much of the Fens was terminated and drainage works were neglected. An Elizabethan survey of Thorney refers to "16,000 acres of fen ground ... which in memory have been dry and firm ... now surrounded (for the most part) by water". The drains had been allowed to become overgrown and silted up.

By the early years of the seventeenth century, however, several quite ambitious schemes were afoot. In 1605 Sir John Popham, the Lord Chief Justice of the day, with a group of associates attempted to drain an area around Upware. They met with various setbacks but eventually constructed a channel from the River Nene system across Fenland to the Little Ouse in Norfolk. This cut retains the name of Popham's Eau.

In spite of ventures such as this, however, flooding seems to have been an increasing problem in the 1620s, perhaps because of the silting up of some of the rivers in the north. In 1631 a group of well-to-do businessmen, led by the Fourth Earl of Bedford, formed the Bedford Level Corporation. The visionary plan was to drain the whole of southern Fenland—parts of Cambridgeshire, Lincolnshire, Norfolk and Huntingdonshire. The group called themselves The Adventurers— they adventured their capital—and those who financed the engineering work received allotments in the reclaimed land. Sometimes one finds these seventeenth century speculators commemorated in the place and field names of the modern Fens— Adventurers' Fen in Burwell parish and again near Haddenham; Adventurers' Grounds Farm, Swaffham Bulbeck. The Corporation engaged the Dutch engineer, Cornelius Vermuyden, who had previously executed drainage schemes in Somerset. His plans were similar to those of Popham and of some of the monastic drainers—the construction of straight, embanked channels, shortening water courses, and carrying the water directly to the sea. His greatest work was the Old Bedford River, a dead straight cut, 70 feet (21.3m) wide and 21 miles (34km) in length from Earith in Huntingdonshire to Denver in Norfolk.

Work was completed by 1652; initially the scheme met with widespread approval. True, there were disputes about the allocation of the reclaimed land and the upkeep of the new channels, but land that had never been ploughed, as far as was known, was brought into cultivation and yielded excellent crops. But within a few decades problems of a much less routine character appeared. The removal of water from the peatlands caused the peat to shrink. Moreover, the continual disturbance of the topsoil by cultivation resulted in the wastage of some of the organic matter by wind-blow and biological action. The channels themselves were lined with silt and so sank less rapidly, so that quite soon the surface of the peat was at a lower level than that of the channels that were supposed to drain it. A vicious circle developed, for the more the shrinkage was countered by more effective drainage the more rapidly the land surface sank. An indication of the rate of peat shrinkage is given by the story of Holme Post. A steel post was sunk into the ground near what was once the south-west margin of Whittlesey Mere, when this, the largest mere of Fenland, was drained in 1851. By 1870 8 feet (2.5m) were exposed and by 1938, 11 feet (3m). A further complication was due to the fact that the northern silts shrank much less than the southern peatlands so that the coastal areas were at a higher level than the peat zone inland. Flooding thus increased.

The introduction of the windpump — a windmill connected to a water-wheel — alleviated the situation. The eighteenth century was the era of the windmill in the Fens, and according to one estimate there were over 700 windpumps operating in the area at the time. Thomas Neale wrote in 1748 that there were over 50 in Whittlesey parish alone. Dr Ennion tells of Adventurers' Fen early this century:

> "Two skeleton windmills did the drainage. They stood half a mile apart, each astride a narrow bricked sluice in which the slatted water-wheel turned when the wind was kind. There used to be more of them but these had been left to rot as the land they drained became stripped of its turf."

The remains of a mill from Adventurers' Fen were transferred to Wicken Sedge Fen in the 1950s. Here, arranged so that water is pumped *into* the fen instead of out into the dykes, it was re-erected and is preserved by the National Trust as the last surviving windpump in the Fens. Alas, it is of no great antiquity and is not entirely typical.

A windmill is a fickle servant, ineffective in calm and at the mercy of gale or frost, and as the lowering of the peat continued into the nineteenth century things became more and more difficult. Arthur Young wrote in dismay of the Fens in the summer of 1805 that in areas that usually supported "great crops of cole, oats and wheat there was nothing to be seen but desolation". He predicted "should a great flood come within the next two or three years, for want of improved outfall, the whole country, fertile as it is, will be abandoned". Once again it was technical innovation that saved the day. The first Watt steam engine was introduced to drive a scoop wheel at Bottisham Fen in 1820. Others followed, so that by the middle of the century there were 64 steam-driven pumps between Cambridge and Lincoln. An inscription on a pumping station built in 1830 reads:

> These Fens have oftimes been by water drown'd,
> Science a remedy in Water found,
> The powers of Steam she said shall be employ'd,
> And the Destroyer by Itself destroy'd.

But the transition from a wet fen community with meadowsweet and yellow flag to fertile fields growing wheat and roots is easily reversed. A short period of neglect and farmland is soon overwhelmed. Adventurers' Fen near Burwell has been reclaimed and fallen back to reedbed several times. From its name it was presumably improved land after Vermuyden's drainage, but it had long been marshland by 1900. It was reclaimed for agriculture in about 1910, but reverted to reeds in the depressed 1920s. By 1941, with the war-time necessity for home-produced food it was again under the plough.

Figure 45. Fenland landscape from the air. The "Washes" with the New Bedford Level or Hundred Foot Drain in the foreground. *University of Cambridge*

The northern part of Adventurers' Fen adjoins Wicken Sedge Fen and is now part of the National Trust property, and it is on this reserve that undrained fen vegetation can be seen most advantageously. The streams from the Chalk country to the east bring lime and thus the peat at Wicken and indeed all of southern Fenland, is alkali in contrast to the acid peats of upland Britain, and thus it supports a much more varied community of animals and plants. But although it is a relict community, an island of nature surrounded by farmland, the vegetation of the Wicken Fen reserve is far from "natural". For centuries the fen was divided into narrow strips where the villagers mowed sedge for thatching and litter for animal bedding or dug for peat. Just as open water is soon infilled by the remains of aquatic plants and then colonised by reed (*Phragmites communis*) and sedge (*Cladium mariscus*), so the sedge fields, if uncut for a decade or so, will be invaded by "carr", a low tangled woodland of birch (*Betula pubescens* and *B. verrucosa*), buckthorn (*Rhamnus catharticus*), alder buckthorn (*Frangula alnus*) and guelder rose (*Viburnum opulus*). Although carr covers part of the fen, present management policies are aimed at cutting the brushwood regularly and encouraging the growth of the sedge which formerly covered much of the reserve. With the current vogue for "doing up" country cottages, thatching is far from being a dying craft, and both reed — used in East Anglia for the main part of a thatched roof — and sedge — for finishing the ridge — command a ready sale in the eastern counties. Both are regularly cut at Wicken and the money received assists with the upkeep of the reserve as a whole. This regular cutting increases the overall ecological diversity of the Fen and encourages the growth of certain smaller plant species.

Figure 46. Cutting rushes, Debenham, East Suffolk, 1955.

*Suffolk Photo Survey (Abbot's Hall Museum)*

Figure 47. Thatching the church at Butley, East Suffolk, 1955.

*Suffolk Photo Survey (Abbot's Hall Museum)*

The visitor taking a summer stroll along Sedge Fen Drove, the main Drove at Wicken, is certain to see something of the rich and attractive fen flora: purple spikes of marsh orchid (*Dactylorchis incarnata*) protrude from the grass and in some of the boggy patches kingcups or marsh marigold (*Caltha palustris*) provide a brilliant splash of gold against the dark, oozing peat. And the floristic diversity of the East Anglian Fens is reflected in the rich insect fauna; over 1,000 species of beetles have been found at Wicken, and 750 species of lepidoptera (butterflies and moths) have been noted. The total number of insect species that have been recorded from the reserve is well over 5,000. Larger organisms are also well represented: the pleasure and interest of a walk at Wicken may be heightened on hearing the tireless reeling of the rare grasshopper warbler, (*Locustella naevia*) or the enigmatic drumming of a snipe swooping and diving over the reedbeds in a display flight.

Figure 48. Marshland bird: the snipe (*Gallinago gallinago*).　　　　　*E. A. Armstrong*

Sedge Fen Drove is probably well over three hundred years old and provided access to the strip holdings where turf was dug and sedge cut. One of these strips, together with another in nearby St Edmund's Fen and a triangular area called Wicken Poor's Fen were assigned to the poor, the villagers of Wicken being allowed to cut sedge there on the third Monday in July. This is not now continued and these areas have become bush covered.

Less well-known than the Wicken reserve, but similar in certain respects, is Woodwalton Fen in Huntingdonshire. More wooded than Wicken, this National Nature Reserve supports a herd of deer. Woodwalton is also well-known for its insects. Especially notable is the large copper (*Lycaena dispar*), a butterfly with burnished copper coloured wings which was formerly quite common in the wetlands of the eastern counties, the food-plant of the caterpillar being the great water dock (*Rumex hydrolapathum*) which grew on the fringes of the now drained Fenland meres. The insect became extinct in Britain in 1851, the last specimen being taken at Bottisham. After one or two unsuccessful attempts at Wicken, a closely related Dutch strain of the copper (the original East Anglian sub-species was unique) has been reintroduced at Woodwalton.

It has already been stressed, e.g. in Chapter Three, that the variety of plants and animals found in a locality is closely dependant on the history of the land's use. An interesting recent study organised by Dr E. Duffey of the Nature Conservancy Experimental Station at Monks Wood compared the spider faunas of Woodwalton and Wicken Fens and related differences between them to the contrasting human use of the two fens over the last one hundred and fifty years. The species list for Wicken includes 203 species, that for Woodwalton 148; 110 species are found in both localities. In a "controlled search" by seven specialists who collected from both areas for exactly the same time on a day in October 1971, significant differences were noted between the two catches. A number of woodland types were found at Woodwalton (*Bathyphantes nigrinus, Floronia bucculenta*), while species more typical of open herbaceous vegetation (e.g. *Bathyphantes pultutus*) were represented only at Wicken. These are relatively common species, but when the whole list is considered it emerges that there are many spiders that have been recorded at Wicken but not at Woodwalton — *Maso gallica, Gongylidiellum murcidum, Saloca diceros.* The explanation may be that Woodwalton Fen was partly drained in the middle years of last century and used extensively for turf-cutting. Carr and woodland cover developed; open fen vegetation is rather restricted. The water-table at Wicken has been maintained at a much higher level. Alder buckthorn (not known at the fen in 1860) has spread as reed and sedge cutting declined, but woodland did not expand to anything like the same extent as at Wicken. Peat-cutting was also probably a good deal less important at Wicken Sedge Fen.

Significant areas of reedbed and fen occur outside the Fenland Basin in other parts of East Anglia. They fringe the Norfolk Broads, to be discussed below, and Redgrave and Lopham Fens that separate the Little Ouse and Waveney systems along the Norfolk-Suffolk border, and now managed by the Suffolk Trust for Nature Conservation provide some of the few areas of wetland in the clay plateau area of High Norfolk and Suffolk. Since they were acquired by the Trust a decade or so ago these fens have been intensively studied and demonstrated to have a varied insect fauna — over 320 species of lepidoptera have been recorded.

The coastal marshes of Suffolk have been attractive to naturalists for rather longer, particularly on account of their bird life. Reedbeds occupy the lower parts of the valleys of several of the rivers of east Suffolk, and although in some ways distinctive — the percolation of salt water from the sea makes them somewhat brackish — in many respects the marshes round Easton Broad, Westwood and Dingle Marshes near Walberswick and Minsmere resemble the inland fens in their land-use history and ecology. They have long been used for the cutting of reed and sedge; C. B. Ticehurst quotes documents showing that a substantial sum was paid for reeds and rushes for thatching in the parish of Theberton in 1293 and the cutters with their scythes and wading boots are still a frequent sight in some of the coastal marshes.

The story of the reclamation of the coastal marshes is a long one. The small areas of meadow recorded in the Domesday survey probably represent some local improvement, but there seems to have been little attempt before the conquest at reclamation on any scale. However, between the eleventh century and 1600 quite large areas of marsh were claimed both from "freshwater" marshland areas and the adjoining saltings. The King's Marshes at Orford, for example, were reclaimed in 1169 for the protection of Orford Castle. Prior William of Butley was appointed Commissioner for Walls and Fosses in 1478, as he represented one of the largest landowners in the drained marshland area fringing the Alde estuary. Even at this time there was concern for the sea defences, so some of them must have been constructed long before. It was, however, after 1500 that most of the intensive reclamation took place; the Prior of Butley inned a substantial area of saltmarsh between 1525 and 1535; until then it had been "often drowned with sea water and of little value". Sometimes saltmarshes were reclaimed as the result of a co-operative effort by a number of small farmers, rather than by a single large landowner; thus a group of tenants in 1578 reclaimed 247 acres (100ha) at Walton.

Figure 49. Westwood Marshes, Walberswick, East Suffolk. The marshlands were once drained (the water was removed by windpumps such as the one shown here) but have reverted to reedbed.
*Suffolk Photo Survey (Abbot's Hall Museum)*

Drained marshland pastures were complementary to the heaths and arable lands of east Suffolk for several centuries, the sheep grazing part of the time on each of the three land-use types. The channels, sluices and sea-walls required continual and careful maintenance. Thus the Orford Commission of Sewers which was formed by a number of landowners in 1561, appointed surveyors to inspect and report on the dykes and sea defences; any work done was paid for by the landowners with holdings in the marshes in proportion to the size of their property. The Commission was described, in documents now in the British Museum, as working "to the great good of the tenants, owners and farmers having and occupieing marshes and grounds adjoining or near the sea".

Another quite large-scale co-operative venture was that of the Minsmere Levels Drainage Trust; records of this body (now in the possession of a Halesworth firm of solicitors) show that the earliest proposals for the drainage of the Levels were made by Lord Huntingfield and a group of his associates in 1808. An engineer called Bower was asked to prepare a survey and suggest a drainage scheme; his proposals included the erection of a new sluice and cutting a straight, embanked course for the Minsmere River. But Bower's interest soon slackened and he was dismissed in 1811 for negligence! He was replaced by a man named Smith who adopted the main features of Bower's proposal and completed the greater part of it by 1813.

1,600 acres of grazing land at Minsmere, along with many other low-lying areas on the east coast of England were deliberately flooded as part of the defences against Hitler's *Operation Sealion* in 1940. Reedbeds soon became established and since 1950 Minsmere has been managed as a nature reserve by the Royal Society for the Protection of Birds. But in spite of their interest as bird habitats, research has shown that wetlands which have been improved pasture for a period and then "fallen back" to reedbed have a much less varied invertebrate fauna than those that have a less disturbed history. As in the case of woodlands regenerating in former farmland or pasture, many species never find their way back from similar habitats some distance away.

The Broads are shallow expanses of open water in the winding valleys of east Norfolk — those of the Yare, Bure, Ant and Thurne. They vary in size from Hickling Broad, over a mile (2km) in length along its longest axis to tiny land-locked pools like diminutive Alderfen Broad. In some ways the term "broad" is inappropriate, for in only a very few cases do they actually represent "broadenings" of a main river. Instead the Norfolk Broads fall into two categories, the by-passed broads (like Wroxham and Decoy Broads in the Bure valley) that are set away from the rivers and linked with it only by a narrow channel, if at all, and the side-valley broads in tributary valleys (like the Filby Broad system). A nineteenth century visitor, J. W. Gregory described the situation clearly:

"Instead of the river passing through the broads, it kept sullenly aloof from them; as we sailed down the river there was broad to the left of us, broad to the right of us, broad in front of us, but by a series of ingenious twists and turns, it managed to wind through the whole of them, either eluding any direct contact with them or communicating only by a few narrow and overgrown passages."

Many broads are reed-fringed (e.g. Hickling) or are flanked by stretches of alder carr and fen (Barton Broad).

Broadland is of quite outstanding natural history interest and a number of the Broads are now managed by the Norfolk Naturalists' Trust or under a joint agreement between the Trust and the Nature Conservancy. One of the most appealing and typical bird species of Broadland is the bearded reedling or bearded tit (*Panurus biarmicus*), a beautiful but tiny species that would be rather inconspicuous were it not for the "pink-pink" as members of small groups keep in touch with one another as they dart hither and thither amongst the reedbeds. At the other extreme is the marsh harrier (*Circus aeruginosus*), a long-winged, long-tailed bird of prey that, in its search for food, characteristically gives several leisurely wingbeats, and then glides, wings half raised, over the reeds. An even more striking predator, the osprey (*Pandion haliaetus*) has become a more-or-less regular visitor to Broadland over the last few seasons. The breeding ospreys of Inverness-shire are well known, but it is less widely known that an osprey quite frequently pauses for a few days at Hickling Broad while on its migration route, taking the occasional fish (generally a pike) from the broad and then carrying it to the bare prong-like branch of an oak in nearby woodland before consuming it.

The insects of Broadland, too, are interesting: no less spectacular than the osprey, in its own way, is the brilliantly coloured swallow-tail butterfly (*Papilio machaon*), now not found in Britain outside Broadland, although it was at Wicken until a decade or two ago. The curious striped caterpillar feeds on milk parsley (*Peucedanum palustre*) that grows in the fens at the margins of some of the broads.

The elucidation of the origin of the Broads is one of the most dramatic demonstrations in recent years of the value of a "multi-disciplinary" approach to landscape study. Although an artificial origin for one or two of the broads was tentatively suggested in the 1830s, it was not until the combined expertise of specialists interested in the study of landforms, stratigraphy, ecology and local history was applied to the problem in the 1950s that their true nature was explained. Drs Lambert, Jennings and Smith from Cambridge used a whole range of techniques — pollen analysis, borings, air photo interpretation and the study of old maps and monastic records — in a brilliant piece of research that demonstrated conclusively that the broads are the result of the flooding of mediaeval peat-diggings. For a full account the reader must be directed elsewhere, but some of the evidence considered by the group of scholars is summarised here.

Closely spaced bores were put down many feet into the peat and clay along traverses across the broads and into the fens beyond. In many cases these showed that the edges of the basins in which the broads were situated were vertical or nearly so, and these vertical faces cut across regularly bedded layers of peat and clay. In a number of cases steep-sided islands protrude from broads, the deposits beneath these islands being identical with those under the fens adjacent to the broads. Moreover in some broads long, straight and narrow balks of peat run from the margins out into the open water; in certain cases these coincide with parish boundaries. All this would appear to be consistent with the artificial origin of the broads.

Figure 50. Barton Broad, Norfolk, showing the "balks" — elongate promontaries and chains of islands — that formerly formed the boundaries between separate peat-diggings.

*Cambridge University Collection*

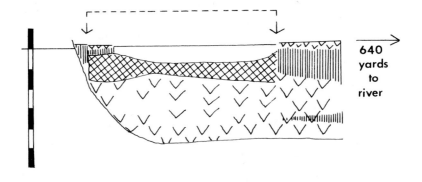

Ranworth Broad — A Simplified Cross-Section

Key

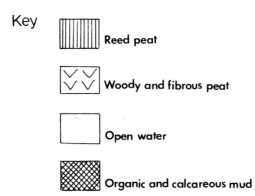

|||||| Reed peat

∨∨ Woody and fibrous peat

Open water

Organic and calcareous mud

Figure 51. Simplified cross-section of a broad in the Bure valley—the arrows show the original extent of the steep-sided depression. Partial infilling has taken place (after Lambert).

Tithe maps made in 1839 provide confirmation of the peat-digging hypothesis. Those of Surlingham Broad and the Rockland/Wheatfen system show boundaries between land holdings on the banks continuing across the open water, suggesting that the whole area was formerly marshland. The parcelling up of Surlingham Broad is particularly elaborate. Further, the Tithe surveys, and also the early Ordnance Survey maps (e.g. those of 1881-4 and 1907) often show long, straight-sided extensions to some broads and sometimes a number of rectilinear water-filled depressions are shown separate from the broad itself. These, in outline and proportions are very similar to depressions that may be seen today in Ireland, for example, where turf is still actively worked.

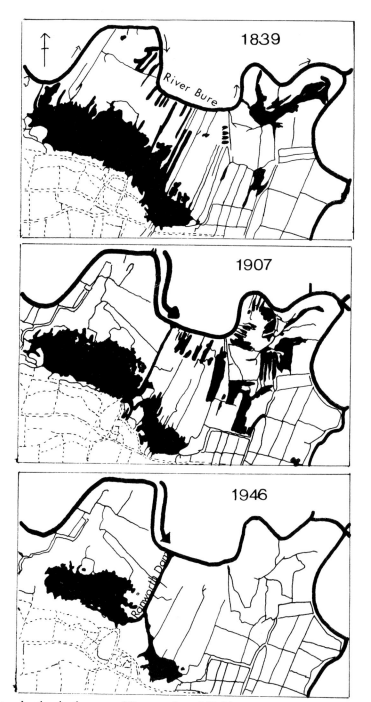

Figure 52. The reduction in the area of Ramworth and Malthouse Broads in the Bure valley, Norfolk as the result of the encroachment of vegetation. The linear outlines of flooded peat-workings can be seen on the earlier maps. The 1839 map is from Tithe Survey documents, that of 1907 from Ordnance Survey maps and the 1946 diagram is based on aerial photography.

The study of still older maps indicates that certain broads were in existence in the sixteenth century and the use of the term "broad" and "water-ground" and references to fisheries in documents suggest that some broads were extant in the 1400s. But there are no references to the existence of large expanses of water in the area prior to the fourteenth century. No fisheries are recorded in what is now Broadland in the Domesday survey, although they are common enough in the west of Norfolk on the Rivers Nar, Thet, Little Ouse and Wissey. However, monastic and legal documents tell of a flourishing turbary (turf-cutting) industry in the twelfth, thirteenth and early fourteenth century. Turf-pits are recorded at South Walsham in the thirteenth century and a note on the sale of tree-trunks from Southfen, Martham in 1320 suggests that the deep "brushwood" peat was being exploited. The gigantic scale of production can be judged from the fact that account rolls reveal that for a time in the fourteenth century 200,000 turves per year were sold from South Walsham. At about the same time diggings belonging to St Bene't's Abbey, Holme, produced 260,000 in one year. Norwich Cathedral Priory was meanwhile consuming some 400,000 turves per year. Norfolk had a relatively dense population in the Middle Ages and on the coast there was a thriving salt industry where turf was used for the evaporation of sea water. The combined demand from the domestic, monastic and industrial users in the area would have been quite sufficient to account for the excavation of the broads in about three centuries.

Towards the end of the fourteenth century the nature of the record changes. There is evidence of increasing flooding and the importance of turbary declines. By 1340 rising water was occasioning serious problems and documents relating to later periods make mention of valuable fisheries in properties that had previously included turbary. Continuity has been maintained, for anglers still come to the Broads to pit their skill against the large pike that lurk at the edges of the reedbeds!

Another fact which emerges when the maps made at the time of the Tithe surveys are compared with those of later date is the striking reduction in the total area of water that has occurred as the result of silting and the outgrowth of reeds and reedgrass (*Glyceria maxima*) from the banks. The amount of the infilling varies; Hickling has not been greatly reduced, but Ranworth has been divided in two. Fritton Decoy, excavated originally to a much greater depth than the other broads, is too deep for vegetation to have been able to encroach and its outline seems to be much as it was 140 years ago. On the other hand Sutton and Strumpshaw Broads have been completely obliterated. The rate of shrinkage has been reduced recently since the introduced South American rodent, the coypu (*Myocastor coypus*) started feeding on the outer edges of the reedbeds, following the escape of a few individuals from nearby fur-farms in 1937. Erosion of the banks by the wash caused by the enormous numbers of river craft that the growth of the holiday industry has put onto Broadland waterways since about 1950 has also prevented further ingrowth.

The broads are far from being the only artificial water bodies in East Anglia. The remains of the moats around ancient farms occur and features largely of twentieth century origin are flooded gravel-pits such as those at Milton in Cambridgeshire or those of the Kennet valley along the Norfolk-Suffolk border. Many of these are now being used by angling clubs, or, where they are partly overgrown, as nature reserves by local Naturalists' Trusts. More interesting perhaps, and certainly more puzzling are the "horned" or "armed" ponds of Cambridgeshire and Huntingdonshire. These pools had a maximum diameter of about 65 feet (approx. 30m) and from three to six arms, arranged like the rays of a starfish around a central area. In Hayley Wood, Cambridgeshire (see Chapter Three) there is a rather distorted four-armed pond whith is about 6 feet (1.8m) deep when full, is steep-banked and has a flat bottom cobbled with erratic boulders from nearby fields. A five-armed example still exists at Dullingham but many others have been ploughed out. They seem to have been quite common over a limited area, for Dr O. Rackham, in a study of estate maps dated 1750, found evidence of 55 multi-armed ponds in 5,400 acres (2,200 ha) in a group of four or five west Cambridgeshire parishes, along with 96 that were round, linear or rectangular. There was a tendency for the latter type to be confined to a single field while the armed variety were often in positions where arms were able to protrude into two or more fields, so it is possible that the ponds were for watering cattle. But with the numerous exceptions to this rule that also existed, together with the fact that some of the pools occur in woodland settings, these ponds remain something of an enigma.

On quite a different scale are the enormous reservoirs made by water supply undertakings. The largest man-made lake in the country is that which covers 2½ square miles of former farmland in the gentle valley of the Diddington Brook between the little villages of Grafham and West Perry in Huntingdonshire. Grafham Water, formed by throwing a dam across the pre-existing valley, contains 13 thousand million gallons of water, pumped from the Great Ouse and destined for consumption by the inhabitants of Luton and Northamptonshire. There was considerable local opposition in the early 1960s (the scheme was completed in 1966) to the flooding of so much fertile farmland and the drowning of several houses, but co-operation from the earliest stages between local planning officials, the Water Authorities and local conservation organisations has produced a landscape feature of quite remarkable amenity and recreational value. Picnic areas have been provided at selected points around the ten mile (16km) perimeter. Sailing is encouraged — the Water is now used for Olympic trials and National championships. The sheltered inlets at the western end of the reservoir, however, are barred to sailing craft, and this part of the Water together with adjoining long-established woodland is managed as a reserve by the Bedfordshire and Huntingdonshire Naturalists Trust by agreement with the Great Ouse Water Authority. Large numbers of mallard, pochard and goldeneye use Grafham Water for wintering and at least eight species of duck have bred in the area. As far as angling is concerned, the plan from the outset has been to provide a game fishery rather than to supplement the coarse fishing already available in the dykes and rivers of East Anglia. Trout (*Salmo trutta*) are introduced at a size of about 1lb (454g) each spring and grow rapidly in the rich water — it contains fertilisers leached from nearby farmland. About 17,000 trout, an average of 25lb/acre (27kg/ha) are caught each year (20lb/acre is considered "good"). However, although Grafham is an artificial environment, artificially stocked, natural ecological relationships apply and fertile eggs of pike (*Esox lucius*) and perch (*Perca fluviatilis*) come in from the river and if the trout fishing is to be maintained, these have to be kept in check. In one recent year 25 tons of perch were removed. About 25,000 anglers visit Grafham each year.

The Breckland meres constitute a group of water bodies as enigmatic as any in East Anglia. They are situated in two gentle valleys, with the steep-sided Devil's Punch Bowl, Fowlmere, Home Mere together with Mickle Mere and the other Wretham Park meres in one, and Langmere, Ringmere, Fenmere and a group of smaller pools in the other. This latter group is now included within the East Wretham Heath Nature Reserve. Teal, gadwall and tufted duck, together with little and great crested grebes are amongst the waterfowl that have bred in this lonely place. Langmere is particularly well-known, its "island" surmounted by a group of eight ancient Scots pine trees presenting an easily recognised skyline. The smaller meres have simple rounded outlines but some have been altered in shape by the digging of marl (Chapter Seven). They may have formed by solution as the chalky till was decalcified by rainwater, rather in the way that swallow-holes have been formed as the result of the solution of limestone in parts of the Pennines. But in view of recent studies of depressions in other parts of Norfolk the suggestion that the meres are situated in ground ice depressions, hollows created by subsidence of surface layers where masses of ice below melted, is also attractive. The hydrology of the meres is almost as mysterious as their origin. The water level in Fenmere, an expanse of water entirely hidden from the casual visitor by a thick tangle of birchwood and scrub oscillates but little, for its depression along with those of one or two other small water-filled hollows, is lined with clay. As a result there is a fairly stable wetland plant community and the flowering rush may be found. The amount of water in Ringmere and Langmere on the other hand varies widely. At times the pine-tree knoll is a true island (e.g. May 1970) but it is more often a peninsula (late summer 1972). On occasions the whole of the Langmere depression is empty (in the autumn of 1964 for example) and is invaded by grass species. Both Langmere and Ringmere were completely dry throughout much of 1973. The level of the water in the meres is dependent on the saturation level in the rock beneath, and there is a considerable delay between rain falling on the surface and its effect on the water-table. Hence the discrepancy frequently noted between the amount of water present in the meres and the weather of the period immediately prior to an observation.

The desolation of the surrounding heathland, the reflections of the lonely pines in the water of Langmere, the shattering of the silence by the sudden splashing, and scurrying as a flight of mallard come down through a hint of an autumn mist onto Fenmere, these are the things that have caused many lovers of quiet places to return to the Breckland meres again and again. A Mr C. J. Staniland visited Langmere in 1887 and described it as

> "...lying in the midst of a wild scrubby heath, not a sound but the melancholy wailing of a peewit or the scream of a gull to break the silence; the dozen or so fir trees on a peninsula standing up in solitary grandeur against the sky. The immediate surrounding of the mere a dried-up, starved stalky growth of thistles and what not."

The planting of so much of Breckland with conifer plantations has reduced the bleakness of the area to some extent, but much of the description is still accurate.

Figure 53. Langmere, Norfolk, full of water.                    *P. H. Armstrong*

Figure 54. Langmere, entirely empty.                            *P. H. Armstrong*

The meres also have considerable archaeological interest. W. G. Clarke, the author of the East Anglian classic *In Breckland Wilds* half a century ago wrote of the same locality:

> "Prehistoric man loved this spot, and strewn all around are thousands of his pot boilers and numerous flint flakes, while on a little plateau across the pool, on the sand of the mouth of almost every rabbit's burrow, there are Roman potsherds of various pastes and patterns."

Since myxomatosis swept the area in 1954 the burrows have become rarer, but the flint fragments can still be found.

At West Mere, West Wretham, when it was temporarily drained for agriculture in the nineteenth century, a circular mound of sand appeared, linked by a wall of marl and flint to a well fenced about with alder stakes. In Mickle Mere, nearby, an artificial island and a structure of oak piles is said to have been found, along with a heap of the bones of deer, oxen and pigs, together with part of a bronze axe. The sites were ill-recorded and the present whereabouts of the finds is not known, but the constructions were probably erected in the Bronze Age when the water level in the meres was consistently lower.

The names Langmere and Ringmere are Saxon, and this may also have been the site of the last great battle in East Anglia between the English and the Danes, in 1010 — the battle of Ringmere Heath (some say that the true location is Rymer, south of Thetford). Many were slaughtered — "Hringmara Heath was a bed of death".

The meres have also long been important as watering places for stock — the importance of the Breckland heaths as grazing areas and the significance of the drove road that skirts the south side of Langmere has already been described, Chapter Five and Six. The boundaries of six parishes converge on Ringmere, giving access to water to the sheep and cattle of several communities. In Fenmere, the timbered remains of a sheepwash, probably dating from the early nineteenth century can be seen.

The drainers of the Fens had a saying: "Is not a fat sheep better than a goose, a stalled ox better than a dish of eels?" Yet in spite of the Adventurers of 1630 and their successors there remain places in East Anglia where the angler, dozing over his line, may look up to see the dark head of an otter furrowing the water, or, closer at hand, a water vole with a youngster in her mouth, swimming to place it in a secure nursery. And although great areas of reedbed have been removed, those familiar with the marshes may still occasionally part the reeds on hearing a loud squealing and glimpse a fat cuckoo chick sprawling on the flattened remains of a reed-warbler's nest.

The scream of swallows wheeling over a pool in which high white clouds are reflected, the striking black and white plumage of an avocet amidst the purple sea-lavender of a saltmarsh — East Anglia would not be the same without trifles such as these.

# CHAPTER NINE

# The Whole Pattern

THE FOREGOING pages have had two rather separate purposes. In the first place an attempt has been made to compile something of an inventory of the components, large and small, of the East Anglian landscape, to draw the reader's attention to a few of the features that together give this distinctive region its character: shingle spit, sea cliff and saltmarsh; hedgerow and field gate; Roman road and milestone — and to say something of the origin and history of some of these things. Secondly, the writer has essayed to show not only that relationships exist between the rocks, soils, plants and animals of the eastern counties, but also that man may be depicted as an integral component of this system. The writer's object has been to show how, for several millennia, man, landscape and living things have interacted, and to demonstrate that the relationships between them are often so intimate that it is appropriately recognised by the adoption of an integrated or holistic approach to the study of landscape. His thesis has been that landscapes should be described as what the ecologist would refer to as "ecosystems"—whole segments of nature. The rocks, soils, animals and plants of a given locality, together with the whole pattern of human activities through the centuries, should be described together rather than separately. Some of the hedgerows of a Huntingdonshire parish may go back to the twelfth century, others may be the result of the activity of an improving landlord just one century ago. The diversity of shrub species found within that hedge will depend partly on the soil and partly on the hedgebank's antiquity. The types of insects, spiders and breeding birds that make their homes within a particular hedgerow are dependent upon its flora and also its management over a period of several centuries. A thorough investigation would require the examination of all these aspects and seek to show the significance of relationships between them.

Thus the investigation of a landscape as a dynamic, functioning system requires the approaches and skills of the local historian as well as the ecologist. The interpretation of air photographs, the scrutiny of legal documents and old maps, pollen analysis, archaeology, stratigraphy, soil studies, tree-ring dating, the field identification of lichens, flowering plants and vertebrate and invertebrate organisms are complementary to one another. Increasingly the enquirer, whether he be a local historian, ecologist or a little of both, is being urged by some of his colleagues to use statistical concepts in his search for relationships and computers for the storage and evaluation of large bodies of data. But these approaches lie largely outside the scope of this book. And where algebraic analysis comes in, aesthetic appreciation is likely to fade away. When a landscape or a community of plants and animals is reduced to a deck of computer cards or a page of calculus something of the wonder of the ecological complexity of an ancient woodland or the beauty of a Suffolk sunset, the stump of an old pumping mill silhouetted against a fiery sky is apt to be lost. It is not always possible to convey the intricacy of the relationship that has existed between a human community and its habitat for thirty generations when, for example, the woodland areas that existed at different dates are plotted on elaborate graphs.

The identification of food-chains and the drawing of food-web diagrams have long been preoccupations of the ecologist, and numerous comments on the food relationships between organisms have been made in the preceding pages. What is often more important, however, is the visualising of a network of ecological relationships in three dimensions. Food and other linkages have a spatial expression; one habitat may be connected to another, nearby or far away. This "girder structure", as Charles Elton called the system by which contrasting communities are locked together, probably contributes to the overall stability of ecosystems. Numerous examples, of various degrees of subtlety may be quoted. The movement of the winter moth caterpillars from the woodland canopy to the soil at the base of the tree-trunk prior to pupation was mentioned in Chapter Two; rather similar is the way in which swallow-tail caterpillars feed upon milk parsley growing in the fens around the Norfolk Broads, the adult butterflies feeding on the pink flowers of ragged robin (*Lychnis flos-cuculi*) the flowering of which coincides exactly with the May emergence of the insects. More spectacular than either of these is the dragonfly which after two years in an aquatic environment as a nymph becomes one of the most aerial of insects, travelling long distances from water. The eel (*Anguilla anguilla*) which was the basis for a distinctive way of life for fishermen in the waterside settlements in the East Anglia of former centuries (three mills at Exning in Domesday Cambridgeshire yielded 7,000 eels per annum) provides an example of an even longer-distance relationship. The link is between the ponds, rivers and streams where the eel spends most of its adult life and the Sargasso Sea where it breeds.

Several ecologists have commented on the rather similar long-distance relationship that exists between the hedgerows and scrublands of the English countryside and the open birch and pine forests of Scandinavia. It has been shown that the principal bird feeders on haws in winter are the fieldfare and the redwing, species that breed in northern Europe. This is important, as these birds are the principal agents of dispersal of the hawthorn, one of the commonest shrubs in lowland Britain. It only requires one shrub of this species to establish itself successfully for a whole colony to be initiated; the birds tend to alight on the growing shrub when it reaches a certain height, so aid further dispersal.

There are important "girders" between hedgerow habitats and other communities much closer at hand. Seven-spot ladybirds (*Coccinella septempunctata*) are often found breeding in arable crops in summer, yet they are likely to have hibernated in a nearby hedge. The significance of this is that ladybirds feed on aphids, which are important pests in cropland.

In Chapter Five it was shown that sheep constituted a vital link between the east Suffolk heaths and the nearby drained marsh and arable lands, grazing on the stubble in the fields after harvest — so adding fertility to the soil — and on the heaths and marshland pasture at other times. Sometimes the sheep were grazed on undrained saltmarsh. Samuel Hartlib's *Discourse on Husbandry* (1651) urged husbandmen to put sheep "into salt-marshes, for in those places sheepe never rot, or ... drive them to a salt river ... and make them drink of the water, this will kill the scab, and also the tickes, and fasten the wooll." Dunes were also occasionally used for grazing. The system was further integrated by the use of "scummings" — dredged material from the marshland drainage ditches — which, when mixed with crag from the pits on the heaths, was used as a fertiliser on the arable lands. It has also been argued that the presence of sheep was important in the maintenance of the grass-covered sea-walls that protected the drained marshland pasture. The suggestion is that the constant cropping of the turf by sheep kept it firm and that the regular trampling tended to fill in the rabbit-burrows and rat-holes. When the sheep disappeared the turf-covered banks gradually became weaker; many of them gave following the abnormally high tides of February 1955, with the result that large areas of farmland were flooded.

It would seem possible that ecological complexity, whether it be the variety that is inherent in a natural community, or the somewhat artificial diversity of a landscape such as that of much of East Anglia, makes for stability. There is now a substantial body of evidence to suggest that highly simplified ecosystems, such as vast single-species conifer plantations or monotonous expanses of arable are unstable: difficulties such as the rapid spread of pests may arise where a single species dominates a community over a large area, and disastrous flooding or soil erosion may occur where the natural, varied, plant cover is removed. For centuries East Anglia has had a landscape of diversity. Man and nature have combined to produce a mosaic of field and hedgerow, woodland and rough ground, copse and heath, broad and marsh. The natural complexity of many of these communities, together with the system of ecological "girders" connecting one with another, and the whole system with areas outside the region, has, in the past, made for a certain harmony and stability in the landscape.

There is a legion of ways in which man has destroyed whole communities of plants and animals and simplified others: the block plantations of Breckland are very different from the natural woodlands that once covered the area and which contained many species of trees. Fungoid parasites and insect pests may spread quickly through the stands of pine. Germinating wheat leaves much of the ground bare of cover in the early part of the year and, particularly in areas where many hedges have been removed, serious wind-blow may result. Nevertheless, there are many ways in which man has increased the diversity of the East Anglian countryside. Although he has drained the great meres of Fenland, in the space of three centuries he carved out a whole new environment in the Norfolk Broads. And while the digging of gravel pits in heathland temporarily destroys an entire community, when the workings are abandoned they present a greater range of microhabitat to reinvading plants and animals than the original flat, open heathland.

One interesting result of ecological research at Wicken Fen has been to demonstrate that although the natural succession—the sequence of plant communities that follow one another as open water is invaded by reed, fen and eventually carr woodland—provides environments for a diversity of organisms, there are certain plants and animals that had no obvious place in this scheme of things. Two botanical examples may be quoted. The fen violet (*Viola stagnina*) was described as "abundant" at Wicken in 1860; by 1910 it was extinct. It survives at Woodwalton, and indeed it is possible to encourage its growth from dormant seeds by removing the carr and leaving a broken peat surface. It seems to require broken peaty ground that remains sodden throughout the winter months, drying out in summer. The violet must have flourished at Wicken while active turf-cutting continued, but declined and disappeared after this ceased. The second example is a charophyte or stonewort (*Nitella tenuissima*), which, although formerly found at Wicken had not been recorded for a long period until it appeared in 1957 in a group of experimental peat diggings made in the early 1950s. Certain species are, and have been within historic times, dependent on microhabitats created by man, and survive only where certain specialised types of human disturbance continue.

Traditional land management techniques—turf-cutting, coppicing, hedge-laying, the grazing of sheep on open heathland and their folding on nearby farmland—are to some extent the products of the society that uses them. Were it not for the relatively high density of population in East Anglia in the mediaeval period and the wealth of the monastic houses, the Broads might never have been cut. Conversely the enclosure of the common lands had a profound effect on the social and economic structure of countless villages. One might argue that a landscape has a sociology, as well as an ecology and a history.

The future of East Anglia's landscape is thus dependent upon the society that relates to it. Two distinct trends can be discerned: the first is a growing interest in natural history, a developing concern for the environment and enthusiasm for conservation. It is manifest in the steady increase in the number of nature reserves—statutory and non-statutory—established in the eastern counties, the increasing memberships of Naturalists' and Conservation Trusts, and a growing vigilance on the part of the community where amenity is concerned. But at the same time internal and external economic pressures are tending to make for standardisation—an increase in field size, the removal of hedgerows, the reclamation of small patches of scrubland. Within a generation much of East Anglia could become a vast arable prairie, isolated nature reserves (well fenced and strictly wardened) providing almost the only variety. The ecological dangers inherent in such a highly simplified ecosystem are clear, and the aesthetic poverty of such an environment, with scarcely a tree's silhouette against the sky to break the monotony, can barely be imagined.

"...Unless one merely thinks man was intended to be an all-conquering and sterilizing power in the world, there must be some general basis for understanding what it is best to do. This means looking for some wise principle of co-existence between man and nature. This is what I understand by *Conservation*."

Charles Elton
*The Ecology of Invasions by Animals and Plants*
1958

Figure 55. Beechwoods in Gog Magog Hills, Cambridgeshire. *P. H. Armstrong*

# Bibliographical Notes

### Chapter One

The Regional Memoir: *East Anglia and Adjoining Areas* published by the Institute of Geological Sciences provides a convenient summary. The Geology of the Cambridge and Norwich areas is covered in chapters in the British Association for the Advancement of Science publications *Norwich and its Region* and *The Cambridge Region,* produced for the Association's meetings in 1962 and 1965 respectively. The section on geology in the Norwich volume is by G. P. Larwood and B. M. Funnel, that in the Cambridge Survey was written by C. I. Forbes, with a description of the superficial deposits by B. W. Sparks and R. G. West. An account of the coastal features of East Anglia is given in chapters 9, 13 and 14 of *The Coastline of England and Wales,* by J. Steers (Second Edition, 1964).

### Chapter Two

R. Rainbird Clarke's *East Anglia* in the *Ancient Peoples and Places* series provides an excellent introduction to the prehistoric and early mediaeval archaeology of the region. The British Association for the Advancement of Science's Surveys — *The Cambridge Region,* 1965; *Norwich and its Region,* 1961 — contain useful local studies written by J. M. Coles and R. Rainbird Clarke respectively. J. Iverson's account of the forest clearance experiment described in this chapter appeared in *Scientific American* in 1956 and was republished in *Man and the Ecosphere,* edited by Paul Ehrlich in 1971. W. Pennington's *History of British Vegetation* (1969) contains a number of East Anglian examples and represents an excellent general summary of what is known about the changes in Britain's vegetation brought about at the hand of man.

### Chapter Three

The ecology of woodland communities is beautifully described in the writings of Charles Elton, particularly in his *Pattern of Animal Communities,* published by Methuen, 1966. The *Domesday Geography of Eastern England,* by H. C. Darby, Cambridge University Press, 1957, is the seminal work on land use in the eastern counties at the time of William the Conqueror's survey. An article by R. Lennard was also found helpful by the writer: "The destruction of woodland in the eastern counties under William the Conqueror". *Economic History Review* vol 15 (1945) p. 39. Much of Oliver Rackham's work on mediaeval woodland has been published in the local Naturalists' Trust publication, *Nature in Cambridgeshire,* particularly the 1968 and 1969 issues. He is also author of an important paper: "The history and effects on coppicing as a woodland practise" in *The Biotic Effects of Public Pressures on the Environment,* the report of a symposium organised by the Nature Conservancy in 1968. There are a number of papers on oxlips and primroses in East Anglian woodlands and the relationships between them; the following are important examples: "*Primula elatior:* its distribution in Britain", in *Journal of Ecology* vol 10 (1922) pp. 200-210, by Miller Christy and "Studies of British Primulas II: ecology and taxonomy of the primrose and oxlip" in *New Phytologist* vol 47 (1948) pp. 111-130 by D. H. Valentine. The paper by G. F. Peterken on the "Development of vegetation at Staverton Park, Suffolk" was published in the journal *Field Studies* vol 3 (1969) pp. 1-39. An account of the Forestry Commission's work in eastern England is given in *East Anglian Forests,* edited by H. L. Edlin, H.M.S.O., 1972.

### Chapter Four

Field systems have an extensive literature, and no attempt can be made even to summarise it here. The books in W. G. Hoskins' series *The Making of the English Landscape,* N. Scarfe's *Suffolk* and C. Taylor's *Cambridgeshire,* as well as Hoskins' own title volume, provide pointers. The study of hedgerows has come into vogue as the hedges disappear; useful sources are: N. W. Moore, M. D. Hooper and B. N. K. Davis, "Hedges: Introduction and reconnaissance studies", *Journal of Applied Ecology* vol 4 (1967) pp 201-220, and a booklet entitled *Hedges and Local History,* produced for the Standing Conference on Local History and to which both Prof. Hoskins and Dr. Hooper contributed.

## Chapter Five

The literature on the heaths of Breckland and those of those of the east Suffolk Sandlings is dispersed and there have been relatively few studies comparing the land use and ecology of the two regions. Dr A. S. Watt published an important series of papers under the title "Studies in the Ecology of Breckland" in the *Journal of Ecology*, vols 24-6 and 28 (1936-40). A popular summary is given in the *New Naturalist Journal*, vol 6, (1949) pp 33-40. Several recent studies on the land use of the Sandlings are as yet unpublished e.g. E. D. R. Burrell, *An Historical Geography of the Sandlings of Suffolk* 1600-1850: N. E. Whiting, *Changes in the Agricultural Geography of the Suffolk Sandlings since 1930* — both are London University Master's Degree theses, 1960 and 1967 respectively. The present writer's theses: *The Heathlands of the East Suffolk Sandlings in their Setting: a Systems Approach to Landscape Study* (held in the library of the College of Arts and Technology in Cambridge) is summarised in "Changes in the Land Use of the Suffolk Sandlings: a Study of the Disintegration of an Ecosystem". *Geography*, vol 58, pp. 1-8, 1973 and an article in Suffolk Natural History, vol 15 (1971), pp 417-430.

## Chapter Six

Roads and trackways do not have an extensive literature. W. G. Hoskins *The Making of the English Landscape* (1955) and *Fieldwork in Local History* (1967) were found useful by the writer. N. Scarfe's *The Suffolk Landscape* (1972) deals with the contribution of roads to the landscape of one of East Anglia's counties and a section by J. Liversidge in the British Association *Cambridge Survey* (1965) describes the network of Roman roads in the area. Some work on the natural history of roadside verges and abandoned railway lines has been published by local natural history societies and trusts, e.g. C. W. Pierce and C. E. Ranson "The Conservation of Roadside Verges in Suffolk", *Suffolk Natural History*, vol 15 (1971) pp. 376-388; F. Perring and C. Huxley, "The Abandoned Oxbridge Line", *Nature in Cambridgeshire*, vol 12 (1969) pp 21-22.

## Chapter Seven

H. C. Prince's article "The origins of pits an depressions in Norfolk", in *Geography*, vol 49 (1964) pp 15-32 represents a model for this type of study; Prince shows that many, but not all of Norfolk's hollows are artificial in origin. A paper by B. W. Sparks, R. B. G. Williams and F. G. Bell — "Presumed ground-ice depressions in East Anglia" in the *Proceedings of the Royal Society of London*, A. 327 (1972) pp 329-343 suggests a natural mechanism for the origin of many of the declivities in East Anglia's countryside. R. Rainbird Clarke's *Grime's Graves* (1960) gives an account of the way in which the interpretation of a site may change. Several studies of the colonisation of abandoned pits by animals and plants have been published by local societies; E. Pollard's description of the Roman snail experiment appears in *Nature in Cambridgeshire* vol 16 (1973) pp 25-27.

## Chapter Eight

Prof. H. C. Darby is the authority on *The Draining of the Fens* — his book of that title was published in 1940. A good, up-to-date account is given in *The Cambridgeshire Landscape* (1973) by C. C. Taylor. Dr. E. Ennion's *Adventurers Fen* (Second Edition, 1949) is a beautifully written account of the history and natural history of Fenland. S. M. Walters' account in the British Association's *Cambridge Survey* (1965), provides interesting material on the changes in the ecology of Woodwalton and Wicken Fens over the last few decades, while an article on the spider fauna of these two reserves, by E. Duffey, appears in *Nature in Cambridgeshire* vol 16 (1973) pp 13-18. In an earlier number of the same journal there is a note on armed ponds — vol 11 (1968) pp 25-27. E. A. Ellis' New Naturalist book *The Broads* (1965) is the seminal work on Broadland; this work includes sections by J. M. Lambert, J. N. Jennings and C. T. Smith who conclusively showed that the Norfolk Broads had an artificial origin — their original Royal Geographical Society Research Memoir *The Making of the Broads* was published in 1960.

# Index

Ecosystems, 131, 135.
Edward III, 59.
Eels, 111, 130, 132.
Elder, 31, 64.
Elephants, 12, 22.
Elizabeth I, 59.
Elm, 23, 24, 26, 33, 38, 40, 64, 69, 70, 111.
— — decline, 24.
Elton, C. 132, 135.
Elveden, 75, 88, 92.
Ely Cathedral, 47, 108, 112.
Enclosures, 59-66, 99.
Ennion, E. A. R., 26, 111, 114.
Eriswell, 80, 86, 89.
Erosion, 19, 75.
Erratics, 14.
Everlasting pea, 40.
Eyke, 51, 60.

**F**

Faden, W., 38.
Fakenham, 102.
Falconers' Society, 89.
Fens, 24, 30, 72, 99, 111-119, 130, 133.
Fen violet, 134.
Ferns, 101.
Fertiliser, 12, 67, 70, 83, 128.
Fieldfare, 65, 132.
Field-names, 40.
Field southernwood, 100.
Fire, 22, 54, 70, 87, 89, 90.
Firewood, 69.
Fisheries, 126, 128.
First Land Utilisation Survey, 77, 87.
Flandrian, 23.
Flax, 95, 109.
Flint, 9, 22, 24, 25, 94, 104, 108, 130.
— — -faced walls, 70.
— — -knapping, 23.
Flittermere Lodge, 58, 98.
Flixton-by-Bungay, 59.
Flooding, 133.
Fluvio-glacial deposits, 16.
Forestry Commission, 54, 55, 57, 75, 86.
Fossditch, 32.
Foxgloves, 65.
Foxhall, 26.
Framlingham, 81.
Fritillary, 64.
Fungi, 38, 57.
Furlongs, 60.

**G**

Galley Hill, 94.
Gamblingay Wood, 46, 49.
Game, 53, 67, 80, 81, 90.
Garboldisham Heath, 32.
Gates, 72, 73, 131.
Gipping glaciation, 14.
"Girder-structure" of ecological communities, 132, 133.
Glacial till, 14, 18, 102.
Glaciers, 14, 18, 104.
Gloucester Gemot, 35.
Godwin, Professor Sir Harry, 31.
Gog Magog Hills, 29, 51, 92, 95.
Golf courses, 83, 87.
Good Sands, 67.
Gorse, 56, 75, 80, 97, 88, 90.
Grafham Water, 127, 128.
Gransden, 36, 49.
Grasses, 24.
Grayling, 56.
Great Gidding, 58, 98.
Great Ouse River, 22, 30, 32.
— — Water Authority, 127.
Great Yarmouth, 12, 74.
Grebe, great crested, 109.
Greenwell, Canon W., 104.
Green-winged orchis, 64.
Gregory, J. W., 121.
Gross, Samuel, 76.
Guelder Rose, 116.

**H**

Hardwick Wood, 46, 49.
Hartlib, Samuel, 133.
Hawking, 78, 81 (see also Falconers' Society).
Hawthorn, 31, 38, 64, 65.
Hayley Wood, 37, 46, 49, 50, 127.
Heartrot, 57.
Heather, 17, 56, 88.
Heathland, 12, 16, 26, 53, 56, 74-91, 134.
Hedges, 58-70, 96, 131 (see also dating of hedgerows).
Hedge sparrow, 39.
Henry VIII, 52.
Hereward the Wake, 32.
Heveningham, 31.
Heydon Ditch, 32.
Hildersham, 16.

Hockham Mere, 23, 25.
Hockwold cum Wilton, 99.
Holkham estate, 106.
— —Meols, 29.
Holly, 51-53.
Holme-next-the-Sea, 96.
Holme Post, 113.
Holt, 14.
Hooper, Dr Max, 58, 66.
Hornbeam, 23.
Horses, 23, 50, 82.
Hoskins, W. G., 92.
House of Commons Select Committees, 80, 82.
Hoxne, 14, 22.
Hundred Rolls, 37, 51.
Huntingdon Record Office, 44.
Hybrids, 49.
Hydrology, 128.
Hynde, Sir Francis, 46.

**I**

Ice age, 9, 14, 18.
— —wedge, 16.
Icklingham, 75.
Icknield Way, 32, 92-94.
Iken, 72.
Increment borer, 42.
Infield-outfield system, 88.
"-Ing" place-names, 31, 97.
Interglacials, 14, 18.
Ipswich, 23, 74.
Iron Age, 27, 51.
Irrigation, 83.
Isle of Axholme, 60.
Ivy, 40.

**J**

Jackdaw, 110.
Jay, 57.
Jurassic, 11.

**K**

Kennet, River, 22, 127.
Kesgrave, 63.
King's College, 87.
Kirby, John, 74, 105.
Kites, 89.
Knapweed, 65.
Knapwell Wood, 40, 44, 49.

**L**

Ladybird, 132.
Lakenheath Warren, 77, 78, 80, 86.
Langmere, 91, 99, 128-130.
Lapwing, 65.
Large copper butterfly, 118.
Lark, River, 22, 49, 75.
Launditch, 32.
Leaf-miners, 65.
Leighton Bromswold, 66.
Leiston, 36.
Lennard, R., 36.
Lichens, 38, 39, 56, 82, 90, 131.
Lightning, 22.
Linnet, 65.
Little Domesday Book, 35.
— —Eversden, 110.
— —Ouse, River, 22, 75, 92, 113, 119, 126.
Local Government Act, 97.
Loddon, 102.
London Brick Company, 108.
Long, Dr Sydney, 91.
Lowestoft ice advance, 14.
Ludham, 14.

**M**

Macadam, John, 97.
Madingley, 107.
Madingley Wood, 44, 46.
Mammoth, 23.
Manwood, 78.
Maple, 50, 63.
Marling, 9, 104-106.
Marsh, 120 (see also Fens).
Marsh harrier, 122.
— —orchid, 110, 117.
Martlesham, 26.
Meadowsweet, 49.
Meres, 16, 102, 118, 128-130, 134.
Methwold, 80.
Microclimate, 65.
Midland Hawthorn, 40, 60.
Mildenhall, 75, 80.
Milestones, 98, 131.
Millepedes, 33.
Miller's Tale, 104.
Minsmere, 81, 90, 91, 119, 121.
Mistle thrush, 33.
Monastries, 37, 112, 122, 126.
Monewden, 64.